Endgame

ENDGAME

*The Fall of Marcos
by Ninotchka Rosca*

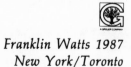

*Franklin Watts 1987
New York/Toronto*

Library of Congress Cataloging-in-Publication Data

Rosca, Ninotchka.
Endgame : the fall of Marcos.

Includes index.
1. Philippines—Politics and government
—1973—   . 2. Marcos, Ferdinand E.
(Ferdinand Edralin), 1917—   . I. Title.
DS686.5.R68 1987   959.9'046'0924   87-15929
ISBN 0-531-15038-0

Acknowledgments

*Like the events of February 22–25, 1986,
in the Philippines, this book is the result
of collective work.*

*Eight researchers collected both firsthand
accounts and reportage of those days.
Clarissa Villasin worked out a chronology
going back to August 1983, when former Sen.
Benigno Aquino was killed. Bobby and Boy
made sure I would get to where I needed to be.*

*My apologies to those whose names could not
be accommodated in the book. When one has
a cast of millions, credits can be tedious.
However, where pertinent, their observations
and experience have been incorporated.*

*N.R.
New York, 1987*

Contents

Endgame

The quality of the highest good is that of water. Water benefits the ten thousand creatures and yet of itself does not contend for its place. It seeks places that men disdain.

Tao: The Way

Chronology

1965   Ferdinand E. Marcos assumes the office of President of the Republic of the Philippines.

1968   Communist Party of the Philippines is reestablished in Pangasinan province.

The Philippine government approves the sending of a civic action group (military engineer battalion) to Vietnam, despite national protest.

1969   Ferdinand E. Marcos begins his second—and by Constitutional fiat, his last—term of office as President of the Republic of the Philippines.

The New People's Army, the military arm of the Communist Party of the Philippines, is established in Tarlac province.

1970   Street demonstrations, strikes and campus barricades, popularly called the First Quarter Storm, erupt all over the country for three straight months.

1971   Two fragmentation grenades explode at the opposi-
       tionist Liberal Party's final campaign rally at Plaza
       Miranda in downtown Manila.

       A transportation strike to protest gasoline price in-
       creases paralyzes Manila.

       A Constitutional Convention is called to modernize
       the country's fundamental legal document.

1972   On September 21, Ferdinand E. Marcos issues Presi-
       dential Proclamation 1081, imposing martial law all
       over the archipelago. Five thousand men and women
       are arrested and held at makeshift military detention
       camps. Newspapers and radio and television stations
       are closed down.

       Rebellion by Filipino Moslems in the Southern Phil-
       ippines erupts. The war eventually drives more than
       a hundred thousand Filipinos into refugee camps in
       Sabah, Malaysia; thousands more are hamleted. The
       Moslem city of Jolo is razed to the ground by the
       military. Middle Eastern countries become involved
       in the war.

1973   A new Constitution is ratified in a plebiscite.

1974   Ferdinand E. Marcos is given a new six-year term of
       office via a referendum.

1978   Elections for the Interim National Assembly are
       held.

1980   Former Sen. Benigno Aquino, in jail since 1972,
       leaves the Philippines for a heart bypass operation
       and eventual exile in the United States.

1981   Presidential elections are held; opposition groups
       boycott them.

The New People's Army numbers ten thousand full-time guerrillas.

Ferdinand E. Marcos assumes his second six-year term of office and his fourth term as President of the Philippines.

1983　The Palace announces that the President will go into retreat "to write two books," sparking rumors that he is critically ill and undergoing a kidney transplant. Former Sen. Benigno Aquino returns to the Philippines; he is gunned down at Manila International Airport.

Salvador Laurel resigns from the Interim National Assembly.

The Philippine currency devalues from week to week; the actual size of foreign loans (at short-term, high-interest rates) becomes publicly known for the first time.

Weekly demonstrations are held all over the archipelago; scores are killed, hurt, or simply disappear as the public and the military clash.

1984　Elections for the National Assembly are held; the opposition wins 30 percent of seats, with 70 percent going to Marcos's party, the Kilusan ng Bagong Lipunan (KBL, or "New Society Movement").

The National Citizens Movement for Free Elections is founded with Catholic Church support.

Armed Forces Chief of Staff General Fabian Ver, twenty-four other military men, and one civilian are accused of conspiracy to assassinate former Sen. Benigno Aquino. Ver takes a leave of absence; Lt. Gen. Fidel Ramos becomes acting chief of staff.

The existence of a secret military organization called El Diablo ("the devil") becomes public. Reports link it to General Ver.

President Marcos disappears from public view for two weeks. Tanks and armored personnel carriers are deployed in Manila. Rumors of a second kidney transplant for the President blanket the country.

The New People's Army numbers fifteen thousand full-time guerrillas.

1985   Cases are filed against General Ver and others. The trial takes one year; all the defendants are acquitted.

Bayan ("the nation"), the largest nationalist-radical coalition, holds its founding congress. Former Sen. Lorenzo Tanada is elected chairman.

Bandila ("the flag"), the largest "moderate" coalition, holds its founding congress. Former Sen. Jose Diokno is elected chairman.

The Reform the Armed Forces of the Philippines Movement (RAM), a secret organization of dissident officers within the military, surfaces. Reports link it to Defense Minister Juan Ponce Enrile and Lt. Gen. Fidel Ramos.

The military guns down twenty-seven peasants at a rally in the sugar-producing province of Negros, where mass starvation has become a way of life. Lt. Gen. Ramos claims the soldiers fired in self-defense. Two hundred sugar workers join the New People's Army after the incident.

The New People's Army numbers twenty thousand full-time guerrillas.

Ferdinand E. Marcos announces during a satellite interview over a U.S. television network that he will advance the presidential election from 1987 to January 1986. Later, he postpones it to February 1986 and agrees to include the election of a vice president. This becomes known as the "snap" election.

Salvador Laurel declares his intention to run for the presidency. The Corazon Aquino for President Movement collects more than a million signatures urging the former senator's widow to run. Laurel and Aquino work out an agreement to form a team under the banner of the United Democratic Opposition.

1986 The campaign begins in January. By the campaign's end, the opposition casualties are estimated at fifty men and women.

Bayan boycotts the election.

The Aquino-Laurel camp holds its final rally at Rizal Park on February 4. The Marcos-Tolentino team holds its final rally at the same place on February 5. Marcos declares February 6 a holiday. Voting proceeds on February 7. On February 8, counting by both the Commission on Elections (COMELEC) and the National Citizens Movement for Free Elections (NAMFREL) are already at wide variance.

On February 9, computer operators at COMELEC walk out, charging discrepancies between tallies of their printouts and the central computer board.

On February 10, the National Assembly constitutes itself into a national board of canvassers to resolve the election returns controversy.

On February 11, the former governor of Antique province is gunned down in public by masked men. Tanks are deployed in Manila.

On February 15, the Catholic Bishops Conference of the Philippines issues a statement denouncing election fraud and terrorism. The National Assembly proclaims Marcos and Tolentino winners of the election.

On February 16, more than a million people join the Aquino-Laurel civil disobedience rally at Rizal Park. The two call for a boycott of all crony-owned corporations.

On February 20, Bayan poises a nationwide people's strike.

On February 21, Scout Rangers arrest the security detail of Trade and Commerce Minister Roberto Ongpin.

On February 22, Defense Minister Juan Ponce Enrile and Lt. Gen. Fidel Ramos announce their secession from the Marcos government. President Marcos accuses the two of an attempt at a coup d'etat.

On February 23, hundreds of thousands of people ring Camps Aguinaldo and Crame to protect the military mutineers. Religious and civic leaders declare support for the rebellion.

On February 24, rebel forces storm the government television station, Channel 4. The air force defects. A crowd repulses attempts by Marcos's troops to penetrate Camps Aguinaldo and Crame. Another crowd rings Malacanang Palace and stones the military men stationed in the area. Defecting pilots fire rockets at the Palace.

On February 25, at 10:00 A.M., Corazon C. Aquino and Salvador H. Laurel are sworn in as President and Vice President of the Philippines. At noon, Ferdinand E. Marcos takes the oath as President of the Philippines. At eight o'clock, he and his family, along with nearly a hundred associates and domestic helpers, are flown to Clark Air Force Base. Two cargo planes take the party to Guam and then to Honolulu. The crowd storms the Palace.

Glossary of Names

AFP   Armed Forces of the Philippines, established in 1908 by the U.S. colonial government. Before martial law, it was limited to the basic services: the Army, Navy, Air Force, and constabulary. After martial law, it annexed the police force. It also maintains the Civilian Home Defense Forces and other paramilitary groups.

Bandila   A coalition of organizations whose political views range from social to liberal democracy, established in 1985; popularly classified as "moderate."

Bayan   A coalition of organizations whose political views range from liberal to nationalist to radical. Established in 1985, it has chapters in almost every province of the country. Popularly known as the "natdems," or national democrats.

COMELEC   Commission on Elections, a governmental institution empowered to oversee the conduct of electoral campaigns and of voting and the tallying of votes. Commissioners are appointed by the President.

CPP   The Communist Party of the Philippines, proscribed by law. It was first established in 1927, was decimated in the 1950s, reestablished in 1968, and is estimated to have forty thousand cadres.

KBL   Kilusang Bagong Lipunan, or New Society Movement, the political party of Ferdinand E. Marcos. It was established after the 1972 proclamation of martial law.

KM   Kabataang Makabayan, or Patriotic Youth. It was established in 1964 and led opposition to involvement in the Vietnam War and to the presence of U.S. bases in the Philippines. Proscribed after 1972, it is the oldest organization allied with the National Democratic Front.

KMU   Kilusang Mayo Uno, or May First Movement, named after the country's official Labor Day. Established in 1980, it is the nation's largest labor federation, with affiliates ranging from hotel workers to sugar and pineapple plantation workers. Its first chairman was arrested twice by the Marcos regime; its second chairman was assassinated after the fall of Marcos. Its political orientation may be gleaned from its self-characterization as "a genuine, militant, and nationalist" labor federation.

Laban	Lakas ng Bayan, or People's Force. It was established in 1978 by former Sen. Benigno Aquino and liberal and radical oppositionists to the Marcos regime. It was concentrated in Metro-Manila and Central Luzon. The Liberal Party, one of the two pre–martial law political parties in the country, it is composed of one wing of the traditional ruling class, the landed gentry. Its name has nothing to do with its political orientation. It was practically decimated by the martial law decree.
NAMFREL	The National Citizens' Movement for Free Elections, a people-based organization established to check and verify the election tally of the Commission on Elections (COMELEC), the official agency empowered by the Marcos government.
NDF	National Democratic Front, an umbrella coalition of revolutionary forces waging guerrilla war. Its membership ranges from peasant organizations to businessmen. Its preparatory commission was established in 1973. It claims control of 20 to 25 percent of Philippine territory and a mass base of 10 million.
NP	Nacionalista Party, the other pre–martial law political party in the Philippines. It alternated with the Liberal Party in control of political power. It is composed of the other wing of the traditional ruling class. Its name also has nothing to do with its political orientation. It too was decimated by the martial law decree.
NPA	The New People's Army, the military arm of the Communist Party of the Philippines. It is

estimated to have between twenty thousand and twenty-five thousand full-time guerrillas. It also maintains a people's militia and the Armed City Partisans. Its composition is estimated to be 60 to 70 percent peasantry. It was established in 1969 in Tarlac province.

PDP The People's Democratic Party, established by former Constitutional Convention Delegate Aquilino "Nene" Pimentel. It was active largely in local elections in the southern and central Philippines, and it eventually merged with Laban forces. The two combined formed the main political organization of Corazon C. Aquino.

PKP Partido Komunista ng Pilipinas, the Communist Party of the Philippines. It consisted of remnants of the old Party established in 1927. It surrendered to Marcos in 1974 and was said to maintain links with the Soviet Union.

PMA The Philippine Military Academy, an elite officer training school patterned after the United States' West Point Academy. Admission is competitive; tuition is state supported. It is located in the resort city of Baguio.

RAM The Reform the Armed Forces Movement, a secret organization of dissident officers linked with Defense Minister Juan Ponce Enrile. Its leadership is mostly composed of PMA graduates. It became public in 1985; its current status is unknown.

UNIDO The United Democratic Party. Founded by Salvador Laurel in 1983, it is the political party under whose banner the Aquino-Laurel team ran in 1986.

ONE

Pathways to Revolt

Toti, age eleven, stoned cars and vans that were flying the Marcos-Tolentino banner, while his sister Alicia, age nine, seeded intersections where Marcos motor caravans were expected with glass shards. It was February 5, 1986, in Manila. From late afternoon to early evening, Ferdinand E. Marcos was supposed to hold a *miting de avance** at Rizal Park. Throughout the day, as Marcos's supporters converged from north, south, east, and west of the city, these children committed their first acts of political violence. One hoped they would be their last.

But this was the Philippines, where in the preceding decade children seemed to have been born cynical; such a hope could only be momentary, fleeting. Toti, smiling with misaligned teeth, clutched with grimy paws a wooden box stuffed with open packs of Pall Mall, Marlboro, and Champion cigarettes, to be sold stick by stick to bus and jeepney

---

* Literally, "advance meeting," a formal presentation of candidates of political parties to the residents of Metro-Manila; it signals the end of a campaign.

drivers for a daily net profit of forty to fifty pesos ($2.00 to $2.50). He was merely one of hordes of children littering the landscape. He was a two-year veteran of the hawking trade at the Katipunan-Aurora crossroads, near the University of the Philippines and Ateneo University. Alicia had debuted the year before as a *sampaguita* flower-garland hawker at the Quezon Avenue–Epifanio de los Santos Avenue intersection.

The street gang's knowing smiles revealed that she could have been doing more than selling flowers. A few weeks before, the sixteen-year-old son of a friend of mine, while visiting Alicia's "turf," had had quite a fright: what appeared to be a ten-year-old girl had offered him oral sex for fifty pesos. According to a male resident of the nearby Heroes Hills District, it would be unusual to find a girl older than fifteen performing in any of the sex clubs dotting the area. Before martial law, this stretch of the boulevard had been residential, an amiable mingling of upper and middle class houses. But the Marcos-supported mayor of Quezon City, Adelina Rodriguez, had approved its rezoning. My friend wondered whether this debasement of the neighborhood had been deliberate; the house of former Sen. Benigno Aquino stood in the midst of the honky-tonks and sex clubs.

My friend's suspicion indicates how easy it was, by this time, to blame Marcos and to see his crudities everywhere. Although Toti and Alicia knew little of politics, let alone what a senator was, they readily asserted that Aquino had been killed by the regime—by the *'dot*, they said, using the short Tagalog form of a four-letter English word. They said this in rhythm, left arms akimbo, right forefingers pointing upward, à la John Travolta. His widow—"*Co-reee!*" they piped, raising hands with thumbs and forefingers extended to form the letter L for *Laban* ("fight on," an acronym for Aquino's political party, the Lakas ng Bayan, "People's Force")—was to be the instrument of their vengeance, the name that would end Marcos's power.

But why did they want Marcos defeated? A pause; side-long glances as if they were shocked and suspicious that anyone would ask. A kid blurted out Mrs. Aquino's slogan: "*Sobra na, tama na, palitan na!* ('Too much already, enough already, replace him already!')." Laughter. Finally Toti ventured, gnawing on his lower lip, "*Mayabang* ('Arrogant')!" Cheers. "*Magnanakaw* ('Thief')!" Cheers. "*Masyadong matagal na* ('He's been there too long')!" More cheers. Alicia added her own analysis: "*Hindi totoo* ('He's not real')!" She was shushed for her naïveté.

The kids' reaction to Marcos's preelection gimmick of reducing gasoline prices was the common one: Why only now, after so long? When it was pointed out that public transport drivers would have more money for cigarettes and flowers, they pursed their lips in disdain. He'll just raise prices again, they said, after victory.

Marcos's economic policy of "demand management"—raising prices to "shrink" demand—was never explained publicly, but the residents of the National Capital Region lived in an environment afflicted by its results. It was a mess. Neither the morning sea breeze nor the evening land breeze could dispel the grayish-blue cloud of dust and carburetor emissions shrouding the business area of Makati and the cities of Quezon, Caloocan, Pasay, and Manila proper, as well as the other municipalities that together comprise Metro-Manila, Mrs. Imelda Romualdez-Marcos's political domain.

A light rail transit system (LRT), built upon her decision, cuts through downtown Manila to neighboring Caloocan. It cost millions of dollars to build, but it was expected to lose money over the next eighteen years. The LRT track looms over the old Avenida Rizal, which had been a children's shopping area—shoes and clothes and toys. It was a dismal sight; the LRT's huge pylons cut off the sun overhead, while soot and noxious fumes hugged the ground below. Suburban residents hardly ventured downtown now, not even to Doroteo Jose Street or the University Belt, which—before Marcos—had been favorite haunts of students searching for cheap, secondhand books. The physical rot of the inner city reflected the political decay. A filthy black canal winding through the downtown's backside was known as "the Estero of Death" after the mangled bodies that occasionally surfaced from its depths—usually corpses of political and community activists.

The tragedy of it, said one old-timer, was that Manila, which had once been a city for children, was now a city for the abuse of children. Writer Ricardo Lee lapsed into incoherent dismay when describing what he had encountered while working on a series of articles on prostitution. He had seen them on the second-floor balconies of movie houses: children peddling their flesh. Male and female. The age of consent appeared to have been reduced to eight years. Hadn't Marcos known? Didn't those around him know?

They must have. In 1980, at an American airport, I came upon a cousin of mine who had married into the Romualdez clan. He was ferrying his son to a school in Boston. By then, most of the children of the rich played, grew up, and went to school overseas. My cousin launched into a self-conscious denunciation of "Filipino values." Bad, terrible, wrong, these values; that's what you should write about, he said. But fortunately that would not be necessary, since the "Ma'am" was aware of the problem. She had decided to do something about it; she was writing a book. With that final sally, he turned and fled, running for the gate to his airplane.

Everyone I told this story to became convulsed with laughter. The "Ma'am," of course, was Imelda Marcos; "Sir" referred to Ferdinand. Even their relatives used these impersonal terms almost as proper names. This depersonalization of Ferdinand and Imelda, from all indications, was not objectionable to them. On the contrary, they had aimed for that status and had carefully cultivated it by a process of self-mythology.

In the beginning, Romualdez clan gossip claimed, the apotheosizing of the Marcoses had been his decision;

Imelda reportedly had had a breakdown or a near-breakdown in her attempt to adjust to the tasteless demands of politics. That was the claim.

Indeed, the Marcos mythology had begun long before Imelda, starting with his story of winning his own acquittal from a murder charge while reviewing for, taking, and topping the bar exams in jail. The story of the twenty-eight medals of honor followed; they had allegedly been conferred on Marcos for leading an incredibly heroic guerrilla group, Maharlika*, during the 1941–44 Japanese occupation of the Philippines. According to a relation of the Ablan family, though, anyone in the Ilocos region old enough to remember World War II knew that there had been only one guerrilla force there and that it had been led by Roquito Ablan, later a pillar of the Marcos regime. "No one will talk about it publicly," said the relative, "but at family reunions, a mention of the Marcos guerrillas brings snickers and guffaws."

If Mrs. Marcos had been reluctant indeed, there was no sign of it. The Marcos political partnership had been seamless from the start. By the late 1960s, the "Sir" was "writing" love poems to the "Ma'am," was building a bridge to commemorate their romance, and smiled benignly at reports that she had exerted near-fatal charms over such world leaders as Muammar el-Ghaddafi and Fidel Castro. Her coloratura singing voice was said to bear no comparison. A Filipina opera singer was once stopped from performing because the "Ma'am" was singing. Perhaps the most egregious instance of her self-mythologizing was a rumor that she was the reincarnation of an Egyptian princess.

The recurring theme of *his* legends was his right, alone, to rule. *By Fate Decreed* was the English title of his film biography, while his book biography, written by two Ameri-

---

* From the words *mahal*, "valuable," and *likha*, "creation." After martial law, though, Marcos's propagandists spread a new meaning for the term: "big phallus." Politically, said some observers, the more accurate translation would be "big prick."

cans, was called *For Every Tear, A Victory.* Destiny and his enduring friendships with all U.S. presidents, both Republican and Democrat, were supposed to be the source of the Marcos magic. But the problem with paragons of perfection, as in the Roman Empire, is that they lend themselves to parody and satire. Street humor added the subtitle "your tear, his victory" to the book, and Manila critics noted an immortal moment in the film biography when, informed that the ailing celluloid Mrs. Marcos was out of danger, the actor playing Ferdinand lapsed into English and intoned "Thanks God!"

Ridiculing the Marcoses was an attempt on the country's part to undercut the danger that they represented. Even before martial law, laughter ran along the brittle edge of fear. When the 1960s segued into the 1970s, the first case of "salvaging" (the military term for kidnapping and execution) occurred. Carlos del Rosario, of the youth organization Kabataang Makabayan ("Patriotic Youth"), disappeared. A few student leaders were arrested.

The decade of the 1970s (in which the number of every year contained his "lucky number," seven) was supposed to be a triumphant period for Marcos. It did not, however, start out auspiciously. Excessive election spending forced a devaluation of the currency—a precondition for stabilization loans from the International Monetary Fund—with the result that the prices of commodities and public services rocketed upward. Popular unrest broke out. Daily demonstrations known as the First Quarter Storm rocked Manila for three straight months as 1970 inched toward a long, hot summer. Protests of Philippine involvement in the Vietnam War combined with protests of domestic policies. Students went on strike and barricaded their campuses. A public transportation strike added to the confusion. No one seemed to know what lay ahead for the country.

It was touch and go whether Marcos would see the end of his presidency. Although he won a second term in 1969, it was supposed to be his last, according to the Constitution. But he was still young, a physical-culture buff, ascetic in tastes; he appeared durable enough, at least in body, to last a thousand years.

In 1971, a Constitutional Convention faltered when Marcos payola for the delegates was exposed; the President had wanted a provision that would allow him to seek another term. As it became obvious that Marcos was looking for ways to remain President, parodying him became a favorite pastime. Stories of his philandering and of his wife's pathetic vigilance were tossed about in newspapers and coffee shops. One had Mrs. Marcos in a helicopter with a pair of binoculars hovering over the golf greens where the "Sir" was playing. An American actress, Dovie Beams, taped her version of love trysts with the President, complete with sounds of creaking bedsprings, moans and groans, and a male voice singing Ilocano songs. Radio stations played the tapes full blast. Mrs. Marcos once explained that the President had managed to save a visiting pope from an assassin; she used the Tagalog word for "left-handed." A terrible howl greeted her statement: the same word meant "cheat" and "philanderer" in slang. She also had to contend with *The Untold Story of Imelda Romualdez-Marcos* by Chit Pedrosa, a work which chronicled the poverty of her childhood.

But these incidents, although good for laughs, did not lessen the sense of danger. Power and money insulated the Marcoses well from self-recognition. Everyone, by and large, was looking forward to the end of his presidency; perhaps then they would become—as Alicia said sixteen years later—less "unreal" and would learn to deal with the country's reality.

One political observer noted that the Marcoses based their vision of the nation on themselves. "Their ability to comprehend the existence of others' needs, others' desires, diminished in direct proportion to their self-indulgence," said Concepcion Aguila. "Towards the end, they were in another country altogether, far from us." Even before martial law, there was evidence that this incomprehension would happen. Scandals linking Marcos to corporations registered in the Bahamas and Antilles had broken out. Vice

President Fernando Lopez, from the bay windows of his top-floor office at the Meralco Building on Ortigas Avenue, pointed to an expanse of land guarded by adobe walls stretching for miles in four directions. The lot had been taken over by Mrs. Marcos without a by-your-leave or thank you to the owners. "Her own Great Wall of China," Lopez said acidly.

Lopez, the Marcoses' erstwhile ally, had come to realize that the First Couple's ambitions went beyond titles and office. He saw that they would use state power to propel themselves to the economic level of the country's richest families. The five hundred or so wealthy families who controlled the country's resources were all related by blood and/or marriage. Any upstart attempt at economic supremacy would displace a fraction of the traditional ruling class. Ironically, it was the Lopez-led enclave that had paved the way for Marcos.

After the sugar barons' bloc pledged their support to Marcos, it was a simple matter to arrange his transfer, in 1964, from the Liberal Party to the Nacionalista Party. It was as simple as his change of religious affiliation, from the minority Aglipayan faith to the Catholic Church. How the political establishment—and indeed, the national electorate—countenanced such cynicism is inexplicable. But it was in keeping with the country's largely feudal political history, whereby backroom deals, shrewdness, personal charisma, and money meant more than principles. In such a setup, the most clever flim-flam man was the logical victor. Perhaps, too, the very singlemindedness of Marcos's obsession disarmed older and wiser politicians.

It seemed during the late sixties and early seventies that after the error that was Marcos the powers of government would revert to either of two young men of impeccable political and social backgrounds: Benigno Aquino, Jr., or Salvador H. Laurel. Both had popular nicknames—Ninoy and Doy, respectively. Both were senators, and both had attended the University of the Philippines, the alma mater of politicians. Aquino had been a newspaperman; Laurel, a lawyer. Both had provincial bailiwicks—Aquino was Tarlac's biggest landlord, and Laurel was Batangas's—and both made no bones about their presidential ambitions. Since they belonged to rival political parties—Aquino was a Liberal and Laurel, a Nacionalista—a contest between the two would be a battle royale.

As Marcos celebrated his second presidential victory, Laurel was hand-picking his campaign's strategists. It seemed an exercise in futility, I told a man involved in that recruitment; Laurel against Aquino would be hardly a match. In fact, anyone against Aquino would be no contest. Just as Marcos had brought backroom politics to perfection, Aquino promised to bring a new style of politics to the country. I was told that Aquino had agreed to let Laurel have the first crack at the presidency, not only because he—Aquino—was younger but also because he himself was averse to succeeding Marcos.

"Not many knew of our long-standing agreement," said Salvador Laurel, laughing. He and Aquino had been close friends since college. After martial law was declared and the Constitution changed, the two decided to try for 1980. "He was going to be my campaign manager," Laurel explained. "We were going to unite the opposition against Marcos." But in 1979 Aquino had to fly from jail to the United States for heart surgery; the stress of seven years' imprisonment and months of a hunger strike had taken its toll.

Then, "when the 1984 parliament elections came around, Ninoy [Aquino] decided it was time to come home. That's why he came home—for the elections. He was going to be onstage with us—proof that we could be and were united."

But soldiers took Aquino off that plane in August 1983, and minutes later he was face-down on the tarmac with the back of his skull blown off. "There were 28,000 of us at the airport to welcome him home," Laurel recalls. "There were only 2,000 soldiers, but they were bristling with guns. I had to make the announcement about the shooting and then try to calm the crowd. If anything had happened, we would have been massacred. It was a terrible moment. After I got the crowd to disperse, I went with Ninoy's mother, younger brother, and other relatives to look for the body. We were driving from one hospital to another. Finally we heard he was at Nichols—a long way off. It took a long time; they would not release the body to us."

A sense of the momentous gripped him at that instant. "I knew it was a turning point," he said. Apparently, so did Marcos's defense minister, Juan Ponce Enrile, who had turned deathly pale when he heard the news. Enrile had known both Aquino and Laurel since college days; in 1971 Laurel had supported Enrile's senatorial candidacy. "He ran as a Nacionalista," Laurel explained, "and I was a Nacionalista." Unfortunately, the Nacionalista Party (NP) slate had been wiped out in that election, the result of a wave of sympathy for the Liberal Party (LP). The LP's *miting de avance* on August 21, 1971, had been grenaded. Many of its candidates were critically injured, but as always those with the least stake in the elections had suffered the most—the audience and media people, scores of whom were killed or wounded. Aquino had been absent fortuitously from the rally, only showing up later in a bulletproof vest and carrying what looked like an M-14.

Perhaps because it was the twelfth anniversary of this 1971 incident, Aquino chose to arrive in Manila on August 21, 1983. Just as, rightly or wrongly, the people had blamed Marcos for the 1971 LP massacre, so too they blamed him for the 1983 Aquino murder.

Aquino dead was difficult to imagine. He had survived imprisonment, isolation, and exile. Throughout the years, he had been the most ebullient and wittiest critic of the Marcoses. A brilliant tactician, he augmented traditional patronage politics with high-tech methods. He once waved some sheaves of computer paper at me, saying they were results of a weekly survey on public response to his speeches. Most politicians at that time gauged their success by the number of column inches they got in the daily papers; this inevitably resulted in meaningless grandstanding.

Spending time with Senator Aquino was an experience in the unexpected. Boyish looking, handsome, and always impeccably dressed, he was nonetheless very 1960s. His informality matched that of post–World War II Filipino baby boomers who had reached or were reaching voting age. He had been about to leave for Indonesia the first time I met him, and he wrecked my composure by offering to smuggle me aboard the plane if I would crawl into his suitcase. Six months later, I peeked into the Senate chambers where a debate was taking place. I winced when he looked up, noted my identity in an instant, yelled my name over somebody's speech, and came dashing up the aisle. Someone told me later that he never forgot a face or the name that went with it. The third time we met, he offered me a lift. While opening his car's rear door, he introduced the man in the back seat as "Commander So-and-So." The man's eyes twinkled; he was cradling what looked like an Uzi. Since the Marcos government was already accusing Aquino of playing footsy with Communists—and even of himself being Commander Dante, head of the newly established guerrilla New People's Army—his words disoriented me totally. I climbed nervously into the car. The man with the Uzi made room hospitably enough. I was eyeing him when Aquino started laughing; the sight of a raw journalist thrust into a "scoop" situation must have been pathetic. The driver laughed; the bodyguard grinned. It was a joke after all, though the gun was real.

A few weeks before, Oplan Sagittarius—a military contingency plan to deal with civilian unrest in the event of martial law—had been exposed. Aquino now expressed his determination not to compromise with Marcos's plans. He would go to the hills, he would launch a movement, he would gather his followers and do—well, "something," he said, gesturing extravagantly, "but certainly, I will not be caught in bed at home." He was already taking terrible risks; he was focusing his public criticism of the Marcoses on Imelda, who, if family gossip were to be believed, had become mentally and emotionally unhinged by both the pressure and privilege of her new status. Because she had married Marcos when he was already in Congress, she had not had the usual political wife's opportunity to immerse herself gradually, at her own pace, in her husband's career and lifestyle. She had had to find another model for herself. Unfortunately, the "fashionable" president's wife of the moment was Jacqueline Kennedy. Mrs. Marcos proceeded to redo herself after her image with no thought for how it would match her own country's idea of a First Lady. The result was an inordinate amount of affectation and silliness on Mrs. Marcos's part, which made her an easy and quick target for public criticism.

Former Senator Aquino knew both of the Filipino's taste for the absurd and of their resentment of powerful and extravagant women. Mrs. Marcos provided him with abundant material to entertain the public. On a live telecast after the grenading of the 1971 Liberal Party rally, Aquino told an anecdote about the then-archbishop of Manila, Rufino Cardinal Santos, and the Marcoses. The three, his joke went, took a helicopter and flew over Manila. Mrs. Marcos wanted the cardinal's advice on how to make Filipinos happy. As the helicopter hovered over the city, Mrs. Marcos tossed out one-peso bills. Would that make Filipinos happy? The cardinal nodded. Mrs. Marcos then decided to toss out five-peso bills. Surely that would make Filipinos even happier! The cardinal nodded. Mrs. Marcos then threw out ten-peso bills, saying that people must be delirious with joy now. The cardinal nodded but pointed to Marcos and said, "If you really want them happy, why don't you toss *him* out?" Hardly anyone could even applaud, they were laughing so hard. I sucked in my breath; there was no way, I thought then, that Mrs. Marcos would let him get away with that one.

In 1972, two weeks after the declaration of martial law, after being strip-searched and fingerprinted at the Camp

Crame gym, I asked a woman sitting on the bunk next to mine where they had found Senator Aquino. "At the Manila Hilton" was the answer, "after midnight. Just as the proclamation was being signed. He and all his bodyguards. Can you beat that?" Aquino had headed a list of some five thousand men and women to be placed under immediate arrest and detention. Although rumors had been rife for months, no one actually was prepared for what Marcos had done, partly because Filipinos, a laid-back Sunday people, tended to ignore a difficult problem in the hope that it would go away. Marcos remained.

I was luckier than most on the arrest list. I had had two weeks more of freedom, thanks to my bedouin existence, though I found out later that the military had visited or raided each of my old addresses. Those two weeks had not been reassuring. Despite the overt political crisis—radio and television stations went dead, newspapers disappeared, and the city of Manila, normally the noisiest in the world, was abruptly quiet—no one wanted to acknowledge that there was one. In public buses and jeepneys, passengers sat in the new silence and avoided one another's eyes. When a building surrounded by barbed-wire and guarded by soldiers in combat fatigues came into view, they shifted restlessly and looked askance on the scene. No one ventured a public reaction. On the first payday after the martial law declaration, crowds boiled in the streets, jamming beer gardens, restaurants, supermarkets, and movie houses in search of escape. Not until the situation touched them directly, it seemed, did anyone move.

But eventually, in ways big and small, many vowed to maintain at least a symbolic protest. Former Congressman Ramon Mitra swore not to shave; Cesar Climaco refused to get a haircut. When he was assassinated in 1984, as mayor of Zamboanga City, he had waist-long hair. Others chose to keep September 21, martial law day, which Marcos later decreed to be Thanksgiving Day, in silence. This was not difficult for former political prisoners since they normally took the precaution of staying away from home, family, relatives, and friends on commemorative dates. For some reason the military was usually restive then. There were also "lightning" demonstrations and marches, mostly by students, mass assemblies and meetings, and church masses with liturgies of the oppressed. The network of resistance was not really set up until 1975, under cover of social institutions outside the government. But nothing galvanized the resistance quite as instantaneously, as dramatically, or as forcefully as the murder of Senator Aquino.

"It was bad enough that Ninoy [Aquino] was killed," said Joanne Maglipon, a journalist, in 1984. "But what made it worse was the story they gave out afterward. It was adding insult to injury. It was a bald-faced statement that Filipinos were the most gullible, the most stupid people on earth." Marcos went on record that Aquino had been killed by Communists. That story in itself was difficult to accept; the alleged killer, Rolando Galman, had a record of working with the military and none of being a political activist. But deliberate media neglect of the murder, the cortege, the lying-in, the five-province march—in short, of everything surrounding the killing—further deepened suspicion. While all this was going on, Marcos's newspapers were doing front-page stories on a man struck by lightning. Maglipon herself followed Aquino's cortege to Tarlac but could find no publisher for her story.

As the crisis grew, it affected almost all aspects of Filipinos' existence, from poetry to economics. The regime tried to deal with it as a minor disturbance. Luis Teodoro, then with the president's Center for Special Studies, recalled that middle-level "intellectuals" of the bureaucracy were herded to Malacanang Palace—"all the president's men, as it were," he said wryly. "We didn't know what was going to happen. We were ushered into this room, and there *he* was. Sitting there with his hands clasped on the desk, as though holding on tight to himself. '*Nay, asuwang* [Mother, a ghoul]' was my first reaction. He looked like death warmed over. He was blue-gray, his face puffy. 'Gentlemen,' he said, 'we will ride this one out.' Ride it out? There were mammoth crowds in the streets, and KKK stores [a Mrs. Marcos project] were burning. A virtual *Götterdämmerung.*" Outside were scenes of horror; Teodoro saw a woman weeping in a grocery store. She did not have enough money to buy infant milk formula, which, like most vital commodities, was imported. And since the peso tumbled in value from week to week, the increase in prices was dizzying.

The regime's distance from the reality of the country increased day by day. Santiago Bose, a painter, remembered hallucinatory costume balls that were hosted by the younger stalwarts of the regime. "First came the Halloween party—and this was just after the assassination. Everything was in black—the hall's decor, the guests, the limousines," he recalled, chuckling. "Everything you wanted by way of food, drinks, smoke, and drugs was available." For weeks before, Manila's waterfront slum areas had seen high officials' sons, chauffeured by military escorts, drive in for drug buys. This was followed by a Valentine's Day costume ball—and this time everything was in red. "Decadence," Bose said, "the masque of the red death, while Rome burned and all that." When Bose and his friends showed videotapes of the crowds at the Aquino cortege in the Metro-Manila Commission Building, the Marcos people present kept muttering that the opposition must have had *so* much money, oh so much money, to have been able to buy such a crowd. They could not accept that people came voluntarily, standing in line the whole day for a glimpse of the body at the Sto. Domingo Church wake. At this wake Dr. Mita Pardo de Tavera, whom the regime had driven from her near-lifelong post as head of the country's antituberculosis campaign, read the first statement to call for Marcos's resignation. In a matter of hours, the demand spread throughout the country: Marcos resign!

"We would not let the regime forget," Laurel said. "We made an issue of the Aquino assassination. In 1984 we told people, 'If you believe the regime's story that Ninoy was killed by Communists, then vote for his candidates. If you don't believe that, if you believe the regime responsible, then vote for the opposition.' " Despite 2.5 million fake registrants smuggled into the Commission on Election computers by Marcos officials, the opposition won 30 percent of the National Assembly seats. "We held Marcos to it," Laurel said with satisfaction. "And we did it. The 1984 elections were a trial run for the presidential election. Without 1984, 1986 would not have been possible."

TWO

The Widow Rising

In Manila by January 1986, cool efficiency and surprising quiet had replaced heat, dust, and chaos at the Manila International Airport. Only one booth at the Immigration Counter was open to take care of the passengers of a JAL Narita-Manila flight. The international travelers were mostly Filipinos returning for the fourth—and as it turned out, the last—campaign of Ferdinand E. Marcos. From Australia, New Zealand, the United States, Europe, Africa, and the Middle East, Filipinos were winging home, half crazed with certainty that something tremendous was happening, or was about to happen in the land of their birth. The regime would soon be dead.

Perhaps they had read the signs; centuries of dealing with colonizers and their strange languages had made them adept at ferreting out truth in the oblique language or the half-completed gesture. Or perhaps they had simply decided that it would be so. But Filipinos were convinced that Marcos would soon be wiped out. That evening on the JAL flight, they spoke of it cheerfully as flight attendants scurried back and forth serving whiskey and beer. A great sports event, this election; a real "Thrilla in Manila." Da Apo (the father, a Marcos nickname) against Da Widow. Even at the airport, they continued giggling, hoisting their carry-ons and their paper bags as well as the thousand packages of *pasalubong*—homecoming gifts, an old Filipino custom—for mother, father, sister, and junior. These packages had clogged the plane aisle, had driven the flight attendants crazy, and had nearly delayed the flight.

On the ground, though, all conversation stopped when a woman in military uniform appeared. The passengers drew apart, each cocooned in a separate silence. Eyes slyly marked the exits—one on either side of the hall. As the woman in military uniform walked by and passed on, a sigh rippled through the line. Habits of wariness die hard in a country of perpetual crisis.

Outside, signs of the Thrilla were everywhere. Posters and spray-painted slogans covered the facades of buildings, some of which were unfinished, or if finished, empty of tenants. Business was bad. The Selecta Lounge on Roxas Boulevard, once a debutantes' haunt, had been gutted and was never rebuilt; the same with Cubao's mammoth Farmer's Market. Armed security guards stood in front of banks and money changers, clutching high-powered weapons. Intact buildings screamed for paint, for cleaning, for maintenance. Only government structures had a look of neatness. Government now was the biggest employer, feeding a bureaucracy of half a million; it controlled most of the available cash. But organizationally, the government was as gutted as the buildings that were deliberately torched for insurance money.

Since the Aquino assassination, said Luis Teodoro, the regime had had "a fin-de-siècle quality to it." Nothing worked anymore. "Even those who benefited from it were skeptical and made nasty remarks in private," he said. "Everyone—or almost everyone—disliked Mrs. Marcos intensely for her extravagance, her stupidity, and her inability to understand what was happening. Marcos himself was completely unaware of how much he was hated."

But pressure mounted internally and externally—from Washington and the International Monetary Fund—and the feeling of being under siege made the Palace inner circle draw tighter and closer. "The Marcoses made it clear it was time for their people to stand up and be counted," Teodoro went on. "But at the same time, with one eye on the writing on the wall, their people were scrambling for one last financial coup. The infighting was vicious."

Even those on the periphery set up alliances to protect themselves from the war going on in the Palace. Rita Gadi Balthazar, Mrs. Marcos's favorite TV announcer, reportedly allied herself with an Ilocano warlord. "That's why she could afford to be as arrogant as a Blue Lady," said a Palace insider, referring to Mrs. Marcos's retinue, "even though when you come right down to it, she was only a minor functionary." As power was consolidated among a few Marcos stalwarts, the regime's structure of support—already unsteady—crumbled faster under the terrific demands of the Marcoses.

Adrian Cristobal, a Marcos man since 1965, chairman of the Social Security System, a presidential spokesman, and once the Palace's leading intellectual, was exiled to the periphery. The only bona fide writer in the inner circle, he had been something of a writers' patron. He had cared for about a dozen or so writers, funneling government contracts to them and generally trying to prevent their being too much out in the cold despite their political views. In the mid-1970s, poet Jose Lacaba was under torture; around the same time his brother Emmanuel, also a poet, was killed by the military. Cristobal had asked me to check whether Nick Joaquin, the country's leading writer, would accept one of Mrs. Marcos's National Artist Awards. "Tell Adrian to call me," Joaquin had boomed. "I will if they'll let Pepito [Jose Lacaba] go." A bargain was struck, and Lacaba's freedom was purchased with Joaquin's reputation. The event accomplished two things. It set a new standard for what one would pay to get a friend out of the regime's clutches; and it served notice as to the bit of soul Cristobal was keeping beyond the Marcos touch—until, of course, the assassination.

Five poets wrote verses commemorating Aquino's "martyrdom." They published them in a book using funds reportedly from Cristobal's office. "I had to fire them," Cristobal said, "the most painful thing I've had to do. But I had to do it for my own survival. I had to have an answer, in case someone whispered in the Palace about it." He was excoriated in public; worse, he had to justify his action. "No one remembered how long I had kept some of those poets under my wing," he said mournfully. Despite this he fell from grace, largely because of a memo to Mrs. Marcos. A survey his office had conducted showed, Cristobal wrote in the memo, that the public did not take kindly to the "Ma'am's" frequent, long, and fancifully worded speeches. Cristobal also refused the post of minister of information, which made matters worse. "I wasn't crazy," he said. "You accept that, and you get blamed for everything bad said against them." And Cristobal took seriously any censure from Marcos because he was no "panderer."

Panderers, as the word was used by Marcos people, were those who were close to Mrs. Marcos. Not the least among them was Deputy Minister for Human Settlements Jose Conrado "Jolly" Benitez. "A true Rasputin" was how Marita Manuel, once Mrs. Marcos's information aide for Metro-Manila, characterized the man. "He knew all the right buttons when it came to the 'Ma'am,'" she said. In the late 1970s, the "Sir" began abdicating in the "Ma'am's" favor. "I could not understand how he could have allowed the woman to ride roughshod over him, but it might have been an offshoot of his illness." Inevitably, Mrs. Marcos's thoughts turned to the succession. "The idea that she could be president, the conviction that she would be the next president, the absolute certainty that she would be the country's first woman president—that came from Benitez,"

Manuel said. "Worst of all was the belief that *she* was better even than the 'Sir.' "

Manuel herself had been exiled to the periphery for telling Mrs. Marcos, back in 1984, what she felt. According to a Palace insider, Manuel had gone to see Mrs. Marcos one evening when no one else was scheduled to visit the Palace. She had barely arrived—with writer Carmen Guerrero Nakpil—when Benitez showed up, claiming he was just passing by. This was after midnight. Nakpil maneuvered Benitez away and left Manuel with the "Ma'am"—at which point she forthwith suggested that Mrs. Marcos resign from the Human Settlements Ministry. All the projects for which Mrs. Marcos had been damned were under that ministry: the Bliss housing; the Film Center, whose construction had been marred by an accident that reportedly killed more than a hundred workers; government corporate subsidiaries that went bankrupt after a year or two while people walked away with government money; and so on, ad infinitum. As she spoke, Benitez came knocking at the door, and as soon as he stepped in Mrs. Marcos said, "Marita wants me to resign from the ministry." The man became livid. Manuel and Benitez, according to the insider, had a screaming match. Later, Manuel would defend her suggestion by saying that it had been a demand of the World Bank—the ministry's main financier. But it was obvious that Manuel lost. She asked for an overseas assignment; but she returned in 1986 to help out, one last time, in the election.

As early as March 1985, there were speculations that the 1987 presidential election would be held ahead of schedule. Still, Marcos's announcement to that effect in November 1985—made in the course of an interview with American newscaster David Brinkley over ABC television—caught almost everyone by surprise. The surprise announcement gave the election its name and its character; henceforth it was known as the "snap" election.

Cristobal was skeptical, feeling it was an American trap; he was also sure that the regime would cheat on a massive scale, which would make it vulnerable to both national and international condemnation. On the other hand, an election was necessary, and it seemed the best time to hold one. The stagnant economy had resisted all remedies by Marcos technocrats. It seemed that nothing could be resolved until the question of the regime's viability was resolved. Meanwhile, opposition forces were still fragmented, caught in unsuccessful attempts to create a cohesive national organization.

Consolidating the disparate anti-Marcos forces into one organization had become a priority after the Aquino assassination. But two years into the effort, the results were still nil. The Justice for Aquino, Justice for All Movement had not evolved any perceptible structure. Half a dozen other organizations—the Nationalist Alliance, CORD, and so on—had also failed to become broad-based. Any number of things could account for this phenomenon, including individual ambitions, styles of work, etc. But the basic reason was the near-impossibility of reconciling the interests of everyone who was against the Marcos regime. The middle class had its own objectives in wishing Marcos gone, distinct from those of the peasants, and both women and the urban poor had still another perception of the national situation. The rich oppositionist wing, of course, had its own reasons to wish for the end of Marcos. What could not be resolved was the question of leadership: who could wield effective control of the "antifascist" movement—since that would be decisive in determining what would follow Marcos.

There were clear signs that the regime was giving way at the seams. Wayne Sorce, an American photojournalist, arrived in Manila in time to witness the rebellion of the cadets at the Philippine Military Academy (PMA). "We were at the graduation ceremonies in Baguio City that April," Sorce said, "and the first thing you noticed were these cadets wearing T-shirts and buttons marked WE BELONG. We tried to ask the PMA head—he was a Marcos man, of course—what was going on. He wouldn't say anything, but he was obviously pissed off. Then Ramos [then acting chief of staff] arrived, and the reporters started asking him about the cadets. All he would say was, we should go ask the cadets themselves." At the time, said Sorce, Ramos appeared to be on top of the dissident movement within the military. "There was no mention of Enrile," he recalled, and it was a surprise that the defense minister would later claim the rebelling cadets as his own men.

A few months before the PMA ceremonies, a mimeographed statement, purportedly by disaffected young military officers, had been circulated among the local media, confirming a rumored schism within the military. The statement condemned "the prevailing military culture" that "reward[ed] bootlicking incompetents and banish[ed] independent minded professionals and achievers." It was an obvious reference to Gen. Fabian Ver, chief of staff of the Armed Forces of the Philippines. Ver had been plucked from the reserves by Marcos to serve as his personal security guard and as his chauffeur. As Marcos rose in power, Ver made his way to the upper echelons of the military, becoming head of the Presidential Security Battalion (later expanded to a unit) and the National Intelligence and Security Agency without having acquired either solid combat or administrative experience.

The political nature of General Ver's titles and powers—as opposed to those based on military competence—became obvious when the general, along with twenty-five others, was indicted for complicity in the Aquino murder. Immediately, sixty-eight other generals issued a public statement reaffirming their confidence in Ver. This was followed by the "discovery" of a secret organization within the military called El Diablo ("the devil"). Supposedly composed of some twenty thousand enlisted men, El Diablo was clearly an independent power base for Ver, existing within the military and yet also outside its command.

The We Belong movement, which made its appearance at the Philippine Military Academy ceremonies, shared El

Diablo's nature as a secret and independent power base within the military. The difference was that We Belong was limited to elite officers trained at the Academy, and its allegiance was not to the Ver clique. In a carefully orchestrated "groundswell," We Belong evolved into the Reform the Armed Forces of the Philippines Movement (RAM); its membership eventually included an estimated four hundred junior officers, mostly based in Metro-Manila.

RAM had a ready issue at hand: General Ver's reorganization plan, which would have dismantled the officers' individual power and territorial bases. By setting up regional unified commands, (RUCs) which brought various services of the armed forces operating within a single territory into a single administrative unit, officers were being transferred from one post to another; various battalions and companies were being dismantled and new ones set up. The ongoing dance of commands threatened to disperse tightly knit officers' groups and to undercut General Ramos's control over the Philippine Constabulary. By creating new command positions, appointments to which were the prerogative of the chief of staff, the RUCs also threatened the integrity of province-based commands, including that of Cagayan, Enrile's home province.

Although Defense Minister Enrile steadfastly denied any rift between himself and Ver, his position in the Marcos cabinet was not at all secure. Marcos had announced that the defense minister acted as his liaison with the military only if he had orders to give; otherwise, effective command was with the chief of staff. Ver's 1985 "leave of absence," brought on by the Aquino murder charges, had not eased tensions, since Marcos vowed to reinstate him upon acquittal. Marcos also floated the possibility of creating, for Ver, a ministry of interior with powers over both the police and the military. The defense ministry, said Marcos, would be left to deal with foreign invasions.

Though no specific cause could be cited for the Enrile-Ver conflict, Palace insiders speculated that Ver's expanding powers under martial law were eating into Enrile's prerogatives. At the same time, as the major recipient of aid from the U.S. government, the military was one of the most lucrative centers of government. Millionaire generals were no longer a rarity. The capricious manner in which arrests and seizures were ordered and conducted opened the entire process to corruption. Hardly six months had passed after the imposition of martial law before detention camp inmates became familiar with stories of prisoners paying for their release and for the dismissal of cases—mostly criminal—before military tribunals. The latters' establishment made the process of arrest, trial, and sentencing an exclusive and closed circuit under the military. It was a military tribunal that in 1976 sentenced to death Benigno Aquino, Bernabe Buscayno (the alleged founder of the New People's Army), and Lt. Victor Corpuz (who defected to the NPA in 1969) for subversion.

Personality differences between Enrile and Ver undoubtedly played a role in their rivalry. Ver was a dour, taciturn man who had brought to the regime nothing but his familial loyalty to Marcos. Their quarrel was not helped any by Mrs. Marcos's obvious preference for the general—inspired, said an insider, by the "Ma'am's" resentment of Enrile's wife. A government media woman recounted how in one cabinet meeting, called to discuss the insurgency problem, Mrs. Marcos had "dressed down" Enrile, saying this was his area of responsibility and that he had done nothing at all, accomplished nothing at all, despite the decades in office from which he had benefited greatly. Everyone, said the observer, froze in the face of the "Ma'am's" tirade; Enrile kept quiet, but "you could see from his eyes he was vowing to return the favor at the first opportunity."

Such incidents must have convinced Ver that the succession was firmly in Mrs. Marcos's hands. From all indications, he was determined to keep it there. In December 1984, when Marcos disappeared again for several weeks—for a second kidney transplant, said rumors, since the first had failed—the army chief, a Ver man, fielded tanks and armored personnel carriers in Metro-Manila with impunity.

Ver, according to a government official, had long affected the trappings of a "little president." This official had once seen Marcos off at a domestic airport for a presidential sortie out of Manila. Minutes after the presidential craft had taken off, a second limousine, also flying the Philippine flag, arrived. Officers and soldiers who had broken rank scrambled hurriedly back into line and afforded the disembarking Ver an equal salute of honors as he made for his personal aircraft. The official said that he realized then that the quarrel between the chief of staff and the defense minister —said to be the third richest cabinet member—did not simply involve money but had deeper roots. That the succession was the bone of contention was confirmed by the speed at which Ver's two sons were being groomed for higher commands. In 1985, Irwin, the older son, was to be promoted to general, leapfrogging over his cadet peers, said the official. Only the RAM's overt discontent stopped the promotion.

Like Ver, Enrile was a veteran Marcos man. The difference was that Defense Minister Enrile brought to the Marcos camp a prestigious clan name. He had had to suffer personal humiliation in his fierce loyalty to his political godfather. A personable but rather formal man, Enrile was beginning to show the strain of remaining a Marcos subaltern through the years. Media people and associates complained he had lost his sense of humor and self-irony—of which, before martial law, there had been ample evidence. Back then, he had once met me at his house with the words "welcome to the home of the number-one fascist."

In 1971, he made his only attempt before 1986 to establish an independent political existence by running for the Senate. The candidacy cost him. In the summer of 1971, one of his public relations men contacted me and asked me to convince Nick Joaquin, who was then editor of the magazine I worked for, to write a story on Enrile's origins and childhood. Enrile, it seemed, was worried that the opposition would use the family secret against him. That was far-fetched, I thought then; in machismo land, summer romances and illegitimate children were too ordinary to be scandalous. But since it was a good story, Joaquin agreed; an interview was held and transcribed.

A few days later, the public relations man was back. One of Enrile's people edited the transcript of the interview. Joaquin threw a fit. I had to call Joaquin to reconvince him to do the story; it was still a good one. But revealing his past, as I felt then and as the years showed, was an unfortunate move on Enrile's part. It didn't help his candidacy any, and Joaquin's story, because of its exceptional style, instead of laying the ghost to rest kept it alive. Time and again, the minister was subjected by political observers to amateur, facile psychoanalysis based on the circumstances of his birth. It was subtle cruelty. On the other hand, it did explain why Enrile felt more at home in the Marcos upstart camp than among the old landed gentry, which eventually dominated the legal opposition and the new government.

I had a chance in 1976 to see in a small way how the Enrile-Ver conflict manifested itself within the limits of behavior demanded by their respective titles and positions. The Department (later Ministry) of Foreign Affairs had refused to issue my passport, claiming that the National Intelligence and Security Agency (NISA) was sitting on my application. A check with NISA told me my passport was at the Palace with General Ver. After nearly three months of office round-robins, a colonel finally told me that the general—whom I didn't know from Adam—had vetoed my application, saying that there was no hurry, my trip wasn't official, I should try again later.

I was frantic, of course. I had been tipped off that charges were being filed against those involved in a weapons-smuggling scheme for the New People's Army. During my detention, I had been asked about this. My interrogation had been rather comical since, knowing nothing, I'd ended up asking my "interrogators"—as political prisoners refer to the investigating teams—to tell me what it was all about. They had been eager to answer.

Years later, I found out that an undercover (or in military parlance, a deep-penetration) agent had been unable to recall the name of one person allegedly involved in the operations and had told his superiors that that person had once arrived at a social affair "with Ninotchka Rosca." That was how my name had crept into the whole mess. In any case, since everyone knew that the matter of evidence was of no consequence to military tribunals, the prospect of being hauled before one was worrisome. What a colonel-lawyer of the judge advocate general's office had told me was still fresh in my mind: "Here, you're assumed guilty until proven innocent." Innocence, like virginity, was somewhat difficult to prove. And by this time, having picked my "interrogators'" brains, I did know something after all. I could run for the hills, prepare a massive legal defense fund, or go abroad. Hence, my search for a passport, stymied by a general who was beyond reach.

A friend suggested I see Enrile, who, I was told, was inexplicably recommending the release of a number of political prisoners. I did, expecting him to send me with a note to some minor officer with whom I would have to dicker to see Ver. Instead, Enrile picked up the phone, called the Palace, identified himself as the "Ministro" and asked for "Fabian." Ver was not in. Enrile told the officer to tell Ver to release my passport, saying he would guarantee my behavior abroad. I was nonplussed. Enrile then told me to check with the Department of Foreign Affairs within the week; I was to inform him if there were further problems. I stammered out the hope that I could return the favor someday. "Don't worry about it," he said. "Just behave in a way that will make the country proud of you." Like an idiot, I said, "Well, of course, the country, not the government. The country." Such a look he gave me—I nearly flew out of the room.

The matter became the subject of intense speculation among my friends—all oppositionists. They felt that Enrile must have been aware, first, of how uncontrollable I could be, and second, of how objectionable I found the regime. "He probably wanted to rile up Ver" was the only plausible explanation. Tut tut, they shook their heads knowingly. It seems that a few months before in front of the Palace, Enrile's car, moving to follow the presidential limousine, had been cut off by a vehicle driven by Palace guards. A gun battle was narrowly averted. "Jesus," a resident of a nearby house was quoted as saying, "suddenly, there were all these armed men in uniform jumping from vehicles and taking combat positions. In the middle of the road." But the guards were carrying M-16s, while Enrile's "boys" had only side-arms—so the proverbial cooler heads managed to stop what could have been a one-sided fight.

By 1985, the Palace no longer had a monopoly on passion and tempers. The opposition, composed of between two hundred and five hundred small and large organizations, fought to attain a modicum of unity. "The feeling was," said Wayne Sorce, "that an Aquino had to face Marcos. It had to be the name Aquino." Such poetic justice would appeal to Filipinos, who have a well-developed sense of high drama. "For a while, it had seemed it would be Butz [Agapito Aquino, the senator's younger brother], until he messed himself up," said Sorce. Agapito had been very much in the headlines, leading the "parliament of the streets," until he became too obviously anti-Left, at which point he'd ended up in the cold. "There was that scandalous display at the Bayan congress," said a student who attended the founding ceremonies of the largest opposition group yet. Headed by former Sen. Lorenzo Tañada, the coalition had prestige, manpower, and resources, but Agapito had refused to ally his own August Twenty-One Movement (ATOM) with it, "despite his members' willingness to do so," said the student. "He threatened to expel those who would not leave Bayan—at which ATOM members lost their tempers and said they would expel him. So his organization split. There's ATOM-Bayan and ATOM-Bandila." And Agapito was finished as a unifying force.

"That left Cory," Sorce said, referring to the widow, Corazon C. Aquino. Throughout the summer of 1985 and on into the rainy season, there were innumerable meetings.

Inevitably, someone would say to Mrs. Aquino, "What about you?" "She would go, 'Oh, no. Oooh, nooo,'" Sorce recalled, imitating the widow's gesture—hands flying up, coming down, clasping in front of her chest in her inimitable Alice in Wonderland style.

"It was Ninoy's mother, Doña Aurora, who brought everything together," Sorce said. "She would say, 'Let's talk about this, here, now.' Even the agreement with Laurel. She said, 'All right, let's meet at my house, let's talk about it.' Ultimately, it was the women who brought everything off." To Sorce, it was typically Filipino that women should manage conflicts, think their way through confrontations, and weave a kind of harmony. Backroom politics had suffered a change in the decades of Marcos's rule: they were no longer "gentlemanly" but "ladylike."

There is a rarely printed photograph of Corazon C. Aquino that must have been taken shortly after the assassination. Showing her in her widow's weeds, it is a study in the ugliness of tragedy. Her face is swollen, her mouth twisted. She looks as if a hand had reached out to crumple her face. This—the image of a victim—is instantly recognizable to many Filipinos. Toti and Alicia recognized her picture immediately. "*Kawawa naman* ('The poor unfortunate')," they murmured, clustering for a look. It was uncanny, since the campaigning Mrs. Aquino, with her serene radiance, looked nothing like the photograph. But apart from the murder of her husband, very little else was known about Mrs. Aquino, hardly a murmur—only that she belonged to the wealthy Cojuangco clan and that Marcos's biggest crony of the later years, Eduardo "Danding" Cojuangco, was her cousin. Even those who had met the slain senator or covered his political career barely remembered his wife. The Aquino side of the family had always been louder, more in the public eye.

"There are four things you have to remember about Cory," said someone who had known her before martial law. "Number one, she is very patient. Second, she is deeply religious. Third, she has to be convinced, on her own terms, that what she's being asked to do is right; and fourth, her anger burns slowly but intensely." Ricardo Lee recalled a series of interviews he had with her right after the assassination: "She struck me then as capable of scheming without malice," he said. "Because she is convinced that what she does is ethical, she doesn't feel her actions are directed against an individual in a personal sense."

Others who had hovered about her husband knew her only as the woman of the house who came out briefly to check on their needs and comfort—coffee, drinks, and so on. Those who had been imprisoned remembered her as quiet, self-contained, and uncomplaining. She never spoke about the indignities she had had to undergo when her husband was moved to an isolation cell; according to a woman whose husband suffered the same fate, visitors were strip-searched, and although conjugal visits were allowed, there were closed-circuit video cameras in the room.

There were no indications at all, said Sorce, that Mrs. Aquino was interested in running for president. "Her main concern," he explained, "was uniting the opposition. She was quite sincere about this. That much was obvious." But when her name came up as the candidate to oppose Marcos, there was a "rightness" to it, said a worker. "It seemed better really than having Laurel or anyone else."

"You have to understand the situation," one political science professor said. "By this time, even a dog would have made it as a candidate against Marcos. People would have voted for him, her, or it, merely in protest against the regime. The problem was to turn that disgust into a positive, a mobilizing, force; people had to care if the opposition candidate was cheated. Otherwise, there was no way you could have that final twist that would end the dictatorship. Laurel, unfortunately, wasn't good enough for that. He was a politician. People distrusted politicians. Marcos was one—and it seemed that politicians naturally evolved into dictators."

But Mrs. Aquino was understandably reluctant. Running against Marcos also meant being responsible for what came after victory. Being involved in an opposition movement, or having been the wife of a government official, did not necessarily prepare a person for that kind of responsibility. She set what seemed to be an impossible condition, but in hindsight it was actually the first move toward getting together popular support for her candidacy: she would run only if she were presented with a petition asking her to do so signed by one million Filipinos.

Joaquin "Chino" Roces, publisher of the pre-martial law *Manila Times*, whom the regime had once detained and once placed under house arrest, became the prime mover of the Corazon Aquino for President Movement (CAPM). Quickly, like an avalanche, the ad hoc organization set up stalls for the petition. At streetcorners, banks, and supermarkets, men and women queued up to sign the letter to Mrs. Aquino. One memorable image of the campaign was a photograph of the elderly Roces, his smiling aristocratic face wreathed by a halo of silver hair, wheeling a grocery cart overflowing with petitions.

The die was cast. Mrs. Aquino hied off to a convent to pray for guidance, while outside her followers stirred uneasily, waiting for news. When she came out smiling, it was a yes all the way. She was going to run. Jaime Cardinal Sin, apprised of the fact, reportedly told Mrs. Aquino she was a Joan of Arc. The problem of resources was speedily solved as volunteers carrying signs asking for contributions to the Cory campaign went into the streets. The grocery cart resurfaced as a paper-bag-laden collection unit. If Marcos had not been worried before, the sight of how Manilans responded to the crude, hand-lettered appeal should have given him nightmares. In all the cities and municipalities of Metro-Manila, of which Mrs. Marcos was governor extraordinaire, speeding cars, buses, and jeepneys suddenly swerved toward the curb, and paper bills and coins fell like a shower of love upon the lone volunteer standing on the sidewalk, holding aloft an A PESO FOR CORY sign.

Marcos, however, could bank on the opposition's remaining divided. Salvador Laurel's party, the United Democratic Opposition (UNIDO), in a national convention, had declared him its standard bearer—crushing all hopes, it seemed, for an Aquino-Laurel team. And although Mrs. Aquino had popular support, she had no national organization. The PDP-Laban Party—a merger of Aquilino "Nene" Pimentel's People's Democratic Party, based in his hometown, Cagayan de Oro, and the slain Aquino's Lakas ng Bayan Party, concentrated largely in Central Luzon—had regional centers but was otherwise small and still in the process of growth. The only organization which could match UNIDO's manpower, structural strength, and territorial range was Bayan. But Bayan wanted the inclusion of certain nationalist demands in the candidates' platform—demands that would have alienated a major faction of the elite opposition as well as stirred the active enmity of the U.S. government.

Laurel himself was adamant. "What could I say to my own people?" he asked. "They had declared me their presidential candidate. I couldn't have just set aside their decision." He had carefully built up and nurtured UNIDO for many years, despite Marcos. Nevertheless, negotiations between himself and Mrs. Aquino were initiated. Laurel made one demand: that she run under the UNIDO banner. But this would have meant dumping the PDP-Laban party, to which Mrs. Aquino was attached by sentiment and close association with its leaders, so the talks collapsed. Marcos could crow that the opposition could not get its act together.

"It was Cardinal Sin who brought us together," Laurel said, denying that U.S. Ambassador to Manila Stephen Bosworth had pressured him into accepting the vice-presidential candidacy. It must have been difficult for Laurel; virtually from birth, he had been groomed by his family for the presidency. But this was a last-ditch effort, done minutes before the deadline for filing candidacy papers. Mrs. Aquino accepted the offer to run under UNIDO; Laurel agreed to be vice president, a largely ceremonial post. "I did it for the good of the country," he said. "The cardinal asked me for this sacrifice. And it seemed that it would be better for everyone to be united behind Mrs. Aquino. No, no, her being a woman did not bother me." Laurel smiled, aware that his home province, Batangas, was known for its macho men.

Marcos seemed unable to deal with the reality of Mrs. Aquino's candidacy, said Wayne Sorce, who was at the Palace shortly after she announced her decision. Accompanying a reporter who was interviewing Marcos, Sorce was treated to a real-life Banquo's ghost scene. "It was a long interview," he recalled, "and I was taking photographs. Pretty soon, it was obvious Marcos did not exactly know who or what we were talking about. He kept using the pronoun *he* when referring to 'Aquino.' Then he would allude to incidents which clearly involved Ninoy, not Cory. He kept correcting himself and then lapsing into the same error.

"It was as though Ninoy was still alive, that he was back. Or at least, his ghost was back—in drag, if you wish. Imelda walked into the room toward the tail end of the interview. She stood there, looking at Marcos with this expression. Pitying him like." Mrs. Marcos walked with them to the corridor as they were leaving. "She treated us to a full tirade against Mrs. Aquino," Sorce said, laughing. "She talked on and on. We couldn't leave." She said what a godawful woman this Mrs. Aquino was. Look what she was doing to the Marcoses. How could she do this to them? "She spoke as though Mrs. Aquino had a strange power, that she was a witch almost, who would do the Marcoses terrible harm." The outburst was occasioned by guilt, perhaps, or fear. But what was there to fear? Already, an official of the Commission on Elections had reassured Adrian Cristobal that everything was "in the bag."

THREE

Hope—difficult to describe—was in the air that campaign month, a period of collapsed time when what should have taken weeks to happen happened within hours. The color yellow was everywhere. Mrs. Aquino had chosen it for her campaign as a reminder of her husband's favorite song, "Tie a Yellow Ribbon." Laurel harmonized with the color green. The Marcos camp chose blue and red. All, frankly, looked terrible on sunburned Filipinos, but that didn't matter. They were colors of affiliation, of commitment, rather than of fashion—and Manila residents in particular, traditional oppositionists, threw themselves into the election-cum-fiesta with frenzy.

The last presidential election had been little more than a sham. With the entire opposition boycotting, Marcos had had to put up his own rival. Now experience, resources, and machinery were being pitted against spontaneous, unorganized, but determined effort. The battle seemed one-sided, but as the campaign got under way, what the statistics had not revealed became obvious: Marcos was the underdog. His choice of Arturo Tolentino as a running mate was hailed as something of a coup and a surprise, but it served merely to embitter a number of ambitious men in his own party. Tolentino, who'd been fired by Marcos as foreign affairs minister, was supposed to be a "maverick," but some who worked in the Palace sniggered that even Mrs. Marcos referred to him as "the jukebox." You know, said the wise guys brightly, press the right button, and you get the right tune. Months later, the elderly Tolentino, befuddled by events, said in an interview that he had agreed to run only because Marcos promised to retire within two years.

But a more grievous error was Marcos's turning over the entire campaign, lock, stock, and barrel, to his children. "They decided on everything," said Marita Manuel, "from strategy to financial management to the distribution of campaign materials." The children, who had grown up isolated from the rest of country, could not recognize and had no respect for the folk wisdom and barefoot shrewdness of old political ward leaders. Veteran Marcos hands were soon complaining *sotto voce* about the arrogance and absurdity of the younger Marcoses. Daughter Imee, who was said to control the Marcos war chest of some seven hundred million (accounts differed as to whether it was in pesos or dollars), tended to watch her decimal points. As a result, bribe money—locally and ironically called "election guidelines"—came either too late or in trickles, depending on how the children saw the importance of a region or a ward leader. Old hands also resented the public "dressing down" Imee gave Greg Cendaña, head of the government's National Media Production Center, a man much older and more experienced than she, and a cabinet minister.

Marcos's campaign strategy proved how alien the family and the regime had become. A mixture of polished Madison Avenue advertising style and vulgar counterpropaganda, of honed professionalism and distressing amateurishness, it failed to attain either focus or momentum. No attempt was made to draw a commonality between the candidates—the regime—and the electorate. Rather, it tended to emphasize the gap between the two. Its initial sally was a series of "New Wave" parties in the plushest Metro-Manila ballrooms. The photographs of the bashes— which were duly covered by the Marcos press—merely served to infuriate a populace already burdened with double-digit inflation and 50 percent unemployment. So did the gigantic, light-bulb-framed Marcos-Tolentino billboards set up in areas plagued by recurrent power outages and astronomical utility costs.

Adrian Cristobal had advised Marcos to take the offensive and focus on Mrs. Aquino's lack of qualifications. "Why?" Cristobal raised his eyebrows. "He had nothing to defend!" But Marcos quickly expanded his line of attack— "not on my advice," the scandalized Cristobal hastened to add—into a vociferous anticommunist and antiwoman line. The first was dreary music, as far as the population was concerned. Since 1972, the Left had virtually been the national instructor in how to fight the regime to a stalemate through collective action. The second produced a tremendous backlash. It enraged Filipinas and embarrassed even those who held to the machismo code, under which, of course, one did not attack women for their "intrinsic" frailty. When Marcos declared that women belonged in the bedroom, he laid himself wide open to jeers that he should say that to Imelda.

While Marcos's technocrats were subjecting Mrs. Aquino's campaign to this quasi-intellectual analysis—criticizing the "aesthetic" composition of her posters—his "dirty tricks department" was spraying red hammer-and-sickle emblems over Aquino-Laurel posters. Traffic islands and building walls blossomed with posters that turned the Laban sign into an obscene gesture: a hand with the thumb and middle finger—instead of the forefinger—extended. Television and radio stations ran commercials of an Aquino imitator confessing to "being weak because I am a woman."

No polls were needed to gauge public reaction to the Marcos campaign. One had only to listen to the clicking sounds coming from houses fronting the narrow city streets and alleys each time a Marcos commercial came on. The placid TV viewer would suddenly shift in his seat, frown, and in inchoate distress reach out and turn the television off. A pause. Then, unable to resist eyeballing the object of his anger, he would turn the TV on again. *Click click click.* The tiny sounds were interrupted by sudden explosions of curses.

Although I disliked the regime intensely, I had thought that my reservations about Mrs. Aquino's candidacy—she had no visible program of government, and the forces she led, at best a hodge-podge of conflicting interests and political views, had not had time to develop a coherent national vision—sufficed to give me some distance from the emotional aura of the election. Wrong. I was not immune. Being Filipina, my emotional level was as high as everyone else's. Each time Rita Gadi Balthazar—whom I had known before martial law—and Ronnie Nathanielsz, the principal anchorpersons of the government broadcasts, appeared on television, I could barely restrain myself from ramming my fist through the screen. Balthazar, like most Marcos regime women, had learned to affect the Imelda Marcos no-expression, regal style, while Nathanielsz, a Sri Lankan whom Marcos had made a citizen, was, like most Marcos men, aggressive, abrasive, and smug. I would try to watch calmly, but then an improbable statement from one or the other would send me seething. By the time I had jumped to my feet in rage, curses were resounding from neighboring houses. Then *click click click.* Fortunately, I had a better source of solace than switching the TV or radio off and on; or clawing to pieces the *Panorama* magazine issue that carried the statement that Marcos had the health and physique that men half his age would envy; or plastering my car, as many did, with signs saying CITIZEN BY DECREE/GO HOME AND PLANT TEA.

The Marcos campaign machinery was superficially smooth and awesome in size, but it was actually honeycombed with structural weaknesses—*butas* ("full of holes"), as an ostensibly Marcos man told me, grinning as he piggy-backed protest literature with Marcos campaign materials on their way to the printing press. The entire government bureaucracy, which Marcos used as his campaign's infra-structure, was shot through with secret dissidents, anti-Marcos elements, and even revolutionaries, all of whom eroded the efficiency of his network, diverting manpower and money into the production of what could be and was used against him. Only at the very top, where campaign policies were decided, was the machinery purely Marcos's. His children, aided by U.S. campaign experts, may have known mass communications methods, but they knew nei-ther the reality in which the election was being held nor with whom they were working. A Marcos-Tolentino Move-ment office I visited turned out to be headed by two persons who could not have been—and were not—Marcos men. They made discreet signals. Along with Marcos materials streaming out of the office for distribution were materials condemning Marcos. And in areas like Bicol province, where "election guidelines" were doled out, the money went straight to the New People's Army.

By contrast, people joined the Aquino campaign with high idealism, a sense of outrage, and the determination that Marcos would end here and now. Their initiative and creativity more than made up for organizational and logisti-cal deficiencies. Against the sleek, full-color brochures, buttons, paper hats, billboards, posters, and T-shirts of the Marcos campaign—basically Western paraphernalia—the Aquino campaign poised hand-lettered signs, mimeo-graphed statements, makeshift yellow headbands, T-shirts, and one image that was soul-searing to Filipinos: white sou-taned seminarians standing on traffic islands, holding aloft crucifixes from which dangled white and gold satin banners bearing the Aquino-Laurel names. Marcos countered with military psychological warfare tactics. Electricity and water disappeared for hours; the newspapers were full of sightings of guerrilla "psychotic killers" in cocktail lounges. The unflappable Filipinos grinned and joked that they must have been playing "Tie a Yellow Ribbon" on the piano.

Despite the government's refusal to give Mrs. Aquino access to the broadcast media, the sheer volume of her campaign materials—made possible by individual contributions and production—simply buried Marcos's propaganda. But materials were the least of it, said Charlyn Zlotnick, an American photojournalist who followed both campaigns up and down the major islands of the archipelago. The crowds who came did more. "Mrs. Aquino was drawing three, four times the number of people Marcos was," she said. "It was pretty obvious he was in trouble. Also, those who came to the Aquino rallies were cheerful and happy; you could see they came on their own. On the other hand, those who attended the Marcos rallies—well, they were pretty grim. Also, Marcos always had his shock troops—the most popular entertainers and movie stars. So at the start of his rallies, there would be tremendous cheers and applause—for the entertainers. And he usually spoke near the end so the entertainers would have the chance to warm up the audience. But what happened was that the crowd would peter out as the hours passed, and by the time he was up there to speak, more than half of the audience had disappeared. Then, too, people barely listened. They were mostly curious as to how he looked—whether he was okay or was really dying or dead. Since his collapse in Pangasinan, people sort of got excited over the possibility of seeing him actually expire on stage."

Marcos's first sortie to the Northern Luzon province was a fiasco. What actually happened was never clear, but Zlotnick said there had been an abrupt change of schedule: Marcos did not show up at the next town in his itinerary. Suddenly, people said he had had to be practically carried to the stage at the last town and had peed in his pants while delivering a speech. Then his left hand had started bleeding. His men had clustered about him and borne him off. Meanwhile, the restless crowd at the following town eyed the portable toilet—standard equipment at Marcos rallies, said Zlotnick—that his men hauled everywhere for his use.

The Palace story was that an ardent fan with long fingernails had scratched the presidential hand—an explanation that did not sit well with those who saw Marcos with his hands heavily bandaged over the next weeks. Whatever his state of health, Marcos in person did not even come close to his bare-chested macho portraits. His face was puffy; his eyes were masked by a bluish butterfly-shaped discoloration. His voice—that famous debater's voice—quavered and rasped, rose and fell in volume. His gestures were stiff and awkward; often, his left hand was immobile. Wearing a drab shirtjac, his "lucky" campaign shirt, he seemed to be in the last throes of exhaustion. Watching this shadow of what he had been, one felt momentary sympathy; and since Mrs. Marcos was invariably behind him, someone would say, "Why doesn't *she* let him step down?" But Marcos gamely mimicked his own old bravura, raised his right hand, and chopped the air. Nearly sprawling facedown on the lectern, he was clearly not about to let go of anything. "They'll have to carry him out of the Palace feet first," Adrian Cristobal used to say in the 1970s, not knowing it was a premonition.

Corazon C. Aquino had had little public exposure, but at her first public speech, the electorate fell in love. It was not that she had anything brilliant or original to say; only that her style of oratory was very different from the rehearsed bombast of Marcos and his clones. To those who had grown weary of politicians, Mrs. Aquino's cool voice, the calmness of her delivery, and the simplicity of her gestures were a relief. Mrs. Aquino may or may not have been rehearsed, but she had a way of personalizing every statement, as if it were addressed especially to each individual in the crowd. Instead of treating her audience as passive receivers of pronouncements, she humanized them. The response was tremendous. As a young woman said, it didn't matter what Mrs. Aquino said. "She could read the telephone directory aloud, for all I care!" she shouted above the noise, and went on applauding a speech whose content no one could remember. Mrs. Aquino also had a knack for responding to a crowd's sentiment. She would step forward amid applause, open her arms as if to embrace the crowd, and end with a double L sign. It drove her audience wild.

But even before that first appearance, they had been prepared to love her. A passionate people, Filipinos had been forced into an unnatural state of helplessness and cynicism by the martial law years. Now, suddenly and abruptly, they dropped their skepticism and returned in a rush to their basic lightness of being, embracing what appeared to be deliverance. The nation wanted to hope. Without prodding, as soon as the Aquino-Laurel *miting de avance* was announced for February 4 at Rizal Park, a million and a half decided to attend, singly or with family and friends. Although the rally was scheduled for late afternoon, people began to stream toward the park at one o'clock. A sure sign that they came on their own was the absence of traffic jams. They used available public transportation; chartered buses and motor caravans would have snarled traffic through downtown Manila. Or they arrived on foot, in a thin but steady trickle. And soon the expanse of land that was the park was filled with a solid mass of people. Nothing like it had happened before in the city of Manila.

Toti and Alicia, my itinerant peddler friends, were there. Toti had managed to hitch a ride on a jeepney that a neighbor had volunteered for the use of the neighborhood's Aquino fans. The passengers had contributed to the cost of gasoline. But Alicia had walked to the boundary between Quezon City and Manila—an exhausting trek that had withered her garlands. She had sold half her wares, given some away, and thrown the rest away. Then she had paid her fare and taken a jeepney to the park. She had nothing to sell, but Toti was doing good business.

He was not alone. Peddler carts of boiled corn and peanuts, candies, and soda pop were parked in strategic spots throughout the park, while yellow T-shirts, yellow Cory pins, yellow headbands, and tiny Cory dolls complete with eyeglasses were laid out on cloths spread on the pavement. Like the rest of the children—hordes of them—who had tagged along with their elders or found their way to the rally, both Toti and Alicia wore makeshift yellow headbands and managed to be near the stage from time to time.

Down below, within a cleared and barricaded space, more than a thousand foreign correspondents made up a sideshow—photographers and journalists, terribly macho with their sun-reddened faces and sweat-patterned shirts. Loaded with still and video cameras, tape recorders, and whatnot, they seemed to be an invasion from outer space. They wore frustrated looks because each time a camera was aimed toward the crowd, everyone struck a pose. Filipinos are self-conscious and tend to clown.

I had made my way to within three meters of the reserved area for the press, and there I got stuck. The crowd was too densely packed; movement was impossible. "Don't try to go further," a man said, "you'll get crushed." I said I had to, that I was making for the press section. He glanced at the press badge pinned to my blouse and raised his voice: "Ahoy, let her through! She's media; she's a friend." His cry was taken up: "Media friends! Media friends! Let the press through!" Walking was impossible, so men reached down, grabbed me under the arms, and hoisted me up. I was passed from hand to hand overhead, then helped over the barrier. They did the same for two companions from the Associated Press. When we were safely behind the barrier, the front section of the crowd treated itself to a round of applause.

It was bittersweet, this friendliness toward the media. They could not have known that for nearly a decade, Filipinos overseas had been knocking on one door after another, trying to get the international press interested in what was happening in the Philippines. The country hadn't been a good story then. But it was now—and as if to make up for the neglect, the foreign press was out in full force. I realized that this might not necessarily be a good thing when, as the crowd thundered the Aquino slogan, one man asked for a translation. Where had he been all this time? He'd just arrived three days ago from Ohio. And how did he expect to cover the election without knowing anything about it? "Hey," he said in self-defense, "I didn't ask for the assignment." He would just ask people in the crowd for translations. But his assumption that all Filipinos were familiar with the English language could be a problem: one foreigner had done that and had received a technically correct but totally wrong version—instead of "enough already, too much already, replace him now," he'd gotten "right already, excessive already, and return him already."

The stage—a makeshift one, since the government had refused them use of the concrete Luneta grandstand—was filled with men and women strutting before the crowd. Agapito "Butz" Aquino arrived costumed in cowboy boots and hat. Shades of Billy Carter! White soutaned priests mingled with skimpily clad entertainers and the Laurel "green" girls, while opposition personalities made announced grand entrances. Mrs. Aquino's *mestiza* contingent—half-breed women of the rich—fanned themselves and pretended not to notice how the crowd stared. They sat or stood within a small clear space, a statement that although they now found themselves in alliance with the great unwashed, they would not become overly familiar with the poor. As the sun turned benign and rendered the scene—leaves of trees, patches of the pavement, what squares of grass could be seen, the red-black hair of men, women, and children—a molten gold, the rally began with an invocation. A hush fell as heads bent; even the trading of souvenirs and edibles stopped. Over a government radio station, a hysterical announcer, lying through his teeth, screamed that the rally's public address system had broken down.

Several times during this rally, I was assured that everything was "in the bag"—not only because of popular support for Mrs. Aquino but also because Uncle Sam had already abandoned Marcos. A labor ministry lawyer, working as a volunteer for the National Citizens Movement for

Free Elections, was convinced beyond a shadow of doubt that the United States would not allow Mrs. Aquino to be cheated. "Not with the USS *Enterprise* docked here!" he said, leaning over as we munched sandwiches at the park's deaf-mute-manned canteen. Everyone seemed to know about the Seventh Fleet's maneuvers, not to mention the names of every battleship, destroyer, and aircraft carrier thereof. I could not convince my listeners that contrary to myth, the press was not privy to the battle plans of the republic. So I just nodded as possibilities were laid out for my verification. The marines would come marching down Roxas Boulevard; ships would lob artillery shells bigger than Toyotas at the Palace; weapons were being distributed; the generals were only waiting for a phone call from the U.S. embassy in Manila.

The U.S. presence—unseen, indeterminate, undefined—was a given of the election, perhaps because Marcos had made U.S. support a pillar of his regime. As far as Filipinos were concerned, the shift in the wind was signaled by Washington's release of Marcos's war records—hitherto unavailable to the public. They revealed finally the spurious nature of his heroism and medals. Added to this, the U.S. embassy was holding too many press conferences, praising the holding of the election, on the one hand, and on the other, citing factors that could compromise the integrity of the election. Then the observer delegation from Washington arrived. In all events that involved Americans in Manila, the thesis was that Filipinos themselves must perceive the election as fair and clean, but the situation made this impossible. The press conferences, the presence of foreign observers, and the demands that the government institute "safeguards" already presumed that Marcos would cheat. They also ensured that he would be severely condemned.

How desperate the Marcos camp was, in the final weeks of the campaign, was reflected in the vociferous anti-Americanism of its press. It was funny to see people who for two decades had boasted of U.S. support frothing at the mouth. "The mills of politics," said an amused university professor, "grind exceedingly slow but exceedingly fine." Shrillness could not cover up the fact that the machinery was stalled, that nothing, nothing was working. By February 5, when the Marcos *miting de avance* rolled around, it was all over except for the fireworks.

According to the Aquino campaigners, nothing had been planned to counter the Marcos rally. As it turned out, nothing was necessary. First, the day dawned overcast, with heavy orange-streaked clouds bunching at the horizon. In the streets, men and women eyed the sky expectantly. Marcos's airplanes had been seeding clouds since Monday, nudging them toward rain, hopefully in time to drench the Aquino crowd. But all luck seemed to have deserted Marcos. The rain fell late in the afternoon of February 5, sending his followers scattering. There were scarcely half a million at the park to begin with; it was neatly halved by the weather.

By noon, Aquino supporters were already lining the roads two or three deep. Holding aloft Aquino-Laurel posters and hand-lettered signs and waving whatever pieces of yellow cloth they could lay their hands on, they razzed the passing Marcos motor caravans. With thumb and forefinger, they made an O for money—a gesture that swiftly gave way to the finger of contempt. "How much? How much were you paid?" they screamed. In a fit of good humor, Marcos's supporters would sometimes scream back, "Twenty!" "Fifty!" "Thirty!" They would then make the L sign surreptitiously.

But as the hours passed, discomfort grew, and so did anger. By midafternoon, irate men were dragging sassy Marcos campaigners off vans when they were halted by the traffic light. Fistfights broke out; Marcos vehicles were pummeled with rocks and stones; empty soda bottles arched toward the center of the road, there to smash into a thousand dangerous shards. Polite yells turned into hisses of *Sipsip! Ssssipsiiip!* ("Bootlicker" or "cocksucker," depending on one's social class).

It had been arranged that I would take a government car to the rally as camouflage. The ominously quiet driver, the government men, and I drove through the street disturbances with mandarin detachment. As we approached the park, the clouds broke, and rain drummed on the car roof. Swarms of men and women bearing Marcos banners scampered. People streamed toward us, away from the park, making for bus and jeepney stops, braving the Aquino stalwarts who were screaming curses and waving yellow cloths. The man in the front passenger seat became restless and started muttering. Then he abruptly rolled down the window and yelled at some Marcos followers, "Go home! You'll catch pneumonia! Marcos won't pay for your medicine." Everyone cracked up.

People sought shelter at the Manila Hotel. Loud with laughter, they jammed the lobby, the rest rooms, and the lounges as they eyed the magnificent decor of the country's prime hotel. They also eyed—venomously—the guests at the coffee shop, and I realized that it was probably the first and only time most would ever step into such luxury. In the lobby a man with a megaphone was trying to get them to return to the park; the President was about to speak. He was ignored. Hard eyes and set lips said they'd already stood through too many speeches. Mrs. Marcos had spoken, weepily, twisting her hands, warning about Communists.

As I approached a group in the hotel, they took one look at the press badge pinned to my shirt and turned away. When I insisted on asking questions, they answered obliquely. "Where are you from?" "From close by." "How many of you came?" "Many." "Why are you here?" "The rain; we're tired." "The crowd's small, isn't it?" "No, no; it was the rain." "Are you going back to listen to Marcos ?" "Later, in a little while, soon." They fanned themselves with paper hats and paper fans imprinted MARCOS-TOLENTINO. Stolid, they went on eyeing the lobby's chandeliers.

Beneath the carnival atmosphere of the snap election was the feel of danger. News from the provinces was dismaying. The bodies of three campaigners in Quezon province had been unearthed, mutilated and decomposing. By the end of January, ten opposition campaigners had been killed. One by one, invitations from friends to come and visit their provincial homes were withdrawn, shamefacedly, hesitantly. Barrios that had never seen political violence were suddenly off limits. "We can't guarantee your safety," friends said. "You'll be a stranger. You'll stick out like a sore thumb." Could I hitch a ride with a military vehicle? I asked. They were horrified. That's the last thing one did in the rural areas. Who would guarantee my safety then? They shrugged, looked away, shrugged again. Finally: "The New People's Army. If they say you'll be safe, then you'll be safe."

FOUR

On the March

In 1968 in Pangasinan province, north of Manila, twelve men and women met to reestablish the Communist Party of the Philippines (CPP). Although I was never told exactly who they were, it is safe to assume that most had come from the youth organization Kabataang Makabayan (KM, or "Patriotic Youth") and were my former schoolmates or friends. The KM had functioned as a combination activist-debating-social club for Filipinos growing up in the 1960s. Since Filipino society had no place for its no-longer-children-not-quite-adult population, the KM was tremendously popular. At its peak, it had twenty-five thousand official members and wielded influence over more than a hundred thousand students and youths, who set the tone for debates on the Vietnam War and the government's domestic policies.

After Marcos declared martial law, the KM was among the first organizations to be proscribed. Its national and provincial committees were forced to go underground as the military arrested KM members throughout the archipelago. That some of the country's most intelligent, articulate, and best-trained young men and women were members of the KM or its fraternal organizations did not make any difference. The decimation of the country's intellectual resources was the result. The only Filipino nuclear physicist went to jail, as did a number of writers, painters, young university faculty members, and so on, along with out-of-school youths, union and peasant organizers, community activists, and even a fisherman or two. All in all, an estimated seventy thousand spent time in one or another military detention camp between 1972 and 1986.

Why intellectuals, who could normally look forward to a better future than most, would take the extreme step of setting up a revolutionary movement is easy to understand. It was a gesture both of desperation and of hope. Since rigid relations, based on property, precluded innovation and creativity, the society had little use for intelligent people. It thrived instead on bureaucracy and brute force. What places there were for intellectuals—relegation to the boredom of academic routine or becoming adjuncts of politicians, as happened to the 1950s intelligentsia—were not acceptable. Jose Ma. Sison, the KM founding chairman, had tried to influence some government officials in the early 1960s, but his ideas had not gone past politicians' speeches. Despairing, he had at one point toyed with the idea of setting up a business—an abhorrent fate for a young poet and political philosopher—and his family, a wealthy Ilocano landlord clan, had offered him capital. But he managed to weld together the KM in the nick of time and never looked back. He was thus in a position to influence the ideas of the baby boomers who, restless with the lives of their parents, had given up on tradition as a provider of guidance and direction.

In 1986, when I drew up a list of friends I wanted to see upon my return from exile, I was told that to see half of them, I would have to visit cemeteries and prisons; to see the other half, I would have to convene the higher organs of the underground. It was a succinct summary of what had happened to my generation: resistance, death, imprisonment, or the underground. In this warping of our lives, there was only one consolation: Few compromises had been made, and few had made compromises. The ideals we had started out with remained intact.

Eventually, before and after the elections, I got to meet a few. The underground was so secret in Manila that one could meet its representatives in the most public places. Couriers, staff members of the guerrilla military commission, and territorial commission officials of every size, shape, and degree of tan cheerfully munched hamburgers at various McDonald's, had coffee at Jolibee's, and licked sherbet from spoons at ice cream stores. Some had names; others had nicknames; a few were anonymous—a handshake was sufficient as an introduction.

Although most joined me in this junk food orgy by pre-arrangement, Lualhati Abreu popped up without warning; she slid onto the vacant seat before me and nearly stopped my heart when I recognized her. She had escaped from a Marcos prison some years back, and the regime was still looking for her. I set up a four-hour lunch at the Manila Hotel with Josefina Cruz. She had been a co-detainee at Camp Crame, in 1972. Until two weeks after her release, the military had not known she was the wife of Rodolfo Salas. By this time, of course, everyone did, and Salas himself had risen in the military's order of battle and was alleged to be commander-in-chief of the New People's Army and chairman of the Communist Party of the Philippines. I could tell his wife, when she asked why I chose the five-star hotel, that it appealed to my perverse sense of humor. But to meet her husband and another old friend, National Democratic Front spokesman Antonio Zumel, I had to find private houses; their owners prepared sumptuous meals without knowing who their visitors were.

Lualhati Abreu made me understand why it was easy for those on the regime's wanted list to walk around and "see the sights," as they say. Underground people strove for a painful ordinariness, in contrast to the Marcoses' deliberate cultivation of a distinctive and regal air, a look of being apart, exceptional. Abreu's smiling face was no different from the endless stream of faces passing before the glass panes of the restaurant's windows—faces that the equatorial light sketched in tentative, unfinished strokes: delicate lines for the eyebrows, another for the nose, curved lines for the lips. Faces that, at the instant of being perceived, were already forgotten.

The transformation could not have been easy. My friends had been exceptional—young men and women set apart by too much knowledge and forced to ripen by the creeping economic crisis, the Vietnam War, and the great flowering of youth activism in the 1960s. Achieving this ordinariness must have entailed a terrific struggle with the ego, with the legitimate desire of the talented for recognition. Later, I found out it also meant learning the patience of crocodiles, as the old saying goes, to survive the crushing boredom of a rural existence.

That they still had enough of a sense of humor to send me straight from a New York winter to the humid heat and relentless trek of guerrilla territory, about a day's drive from Manila, was reassuring. But I suffered misgivings as a courier spread out his maps. Through blank spaces, a single line—the Marcos highway—meandered. Fernando Magallanes, the sixteenth-century Portuguese who had sailed under the Spanish flag to circumnavigate the globe and had chanced upon the Philippine archipelago, must have had maps like these. He had named the new land the Archipelago of Saint Lazarus and was promptly killed on Mactan Island for intervening in a local dispute.

"The only problems would be here," the courier said, jabbing a forefinger at the map, "and here and here. Military checkpoints. Sometimes they put up one here and here. Once you get past, you'll be all right. We can pick you up here." No names on indicated places, only landmarks: the old tree, a corner store, so-and-so's hut.

Expect the worst, I was told; take two pairs of walking shoes, don't drink the water, and hope it hasn't been raining. It had. We drove along Marcos's pride and glory: what had once been the Pan-Philippine Highway, now renamed for him. As the rain fell, the inferior cement melted into primal elements, producing craters filled with gravel and sand that ricocheted off the car tires and drummed against the car's belly. Where sections of the road were unfinished or had vanished, there were huge red-brown scars of mud, sloping steeply down and up again. An oncoming vehicle would bring us to a stop; the single lane of compacted mud could accommodate only one car. The landscape remained a monotonous pattern of green—rice or grass and coconuts—interspersed with two-story houses of wood, bamboo, or from time to time adobe, bleached white by the sun. When thirst made us stop, store owners displayed a local adaptation of twentieth-century technology; they poured Coke or Pepsi into a polyvinyl bag and stuck a straw into the package.

Travel was motorized only up to a point; then the car was driven back to the city. A road of ferocious mud confronted us. The guide recruited a lanky barefoot boy to carry our bags. He forged ahead speedily, toes gripping the mud, and he was soon lost from sight. We trudged along. Mud sucked at my sneakers. After about an hour, the guide walked to the road's edge and said we were taking a shortcut. The road was impassable from that point on, the mud being knee deep. It had been raining for a week.

The shortcut was a series of 45-degree inclines, going up and down with bamboo poles straddling tiny yet deep creeks and sudden cracks in the earth. Traversing it required first sliding on one's backside, then falling forward to one's knees. After that one crawled up, using hardened indentations in the mud for handholds. Since I had to do this over and over again, I assumed it was normal locomotion for the area—until I saw the guide, who was five hundred yards ahead. Her starched white blouse was as crisp as it had been when we left Manila. I was coated with mud from head to foot—an ignominy made worse when we reached the first zone of safety, a well-kept barrio whose only inhabitant seemed to be a young dark man standing on a grassy knoll waving an M-16, his chest crisscrossed with bandoliers. Only after he'd given a hearty greeting did people spill from the surrounding bamboo houses: men, women, and children. One child looked at me and piped up, "But why are you so dirty?" Everyone let loose the laughter they must have been suppressing. Only the following day was I mollified—one of the seven guerrillas sent to escort us to the interior slipped and landed on his rear end.

Guerrilla zones looked no different from other Philippine barrios, except they were cleaner—partly because of the absence of election campaign posters. There were the usual desultory huts, the footpaths, and the tiny ground-floor stores; dogs and children shared the same malnourished look. But nothing moved, not even a single leaf, without being noted by observant eyes. Three men sifting through peanut kernels in a winnowing basket in the ground floor of a house were introduced as members of the local militia. Hidden by shadows, their rifles leaned against a nearby wall. Later, a ten-year-old boy recited revolutionary poetry. I became aware then of what none of the reports on the New People's Army had revealed: a "guerrilla zone" was merely people.

It had taken nearly a decade to reach this level of organization, according to Jose Luneta, who arrived at our second stop escorted by about ten guerrillas. His smiling, full-moon face, unchanged by the years, loomed over the clatter of guns and ammo, voices raised in greeting, and men and women embracing. I had to hop-skip over many armaments, flung down by guerrillas who looked as if they had gone on forced march, to reach his extended hand. "We survived!" He'd undergone nearly a year of torture and isolation in his seven-year imprisonment. He had lost his wife. A sister-in-law and her child, barely two years old, had been picked up by the military and were never seen again. All his brothers had been arrested.

"You remember when we went mountain climbing?" he asked. I did. It was in Batangas, the Lunetas' home province. For some quixotic reason, a bunch of Manilans, impoverished by the lack of a hometown, had decided to visit there. I remembered the long trek up with Arthur Garcia, dead now, shot in Tarlac province; the icy stream where, while bathing, a lobster had sent me screaming for Ellecer Cortez, dead now, too, shot in Zambales. Who else had been there? Leni—didn't she decide to become a nun when her brother was killed by the military? Annie, too: her husband, Antonio Hilario, had been shot and buried alive in Aklan. The widowed Mariquit, who had been imprisoned. "It's a zone now," Luneta said, placating ghosts.

About five villages constituted the zone we were in—peasant huts and the fields in between, concentric circles of varying degrees of "safety." Originally a settlers' area, it was still peopled by first- to third-generation migrant farmers who had cleared the primeval rain forest, planted coconuts and bananas, and built their huts near waterways. "There was nothing here at all," said an old man, "except monkeys, rattan, and snakes." But that did not prevent Manila-based rich families from securing titles to the land once it was tamed.

It was an archetypal Philippine story. Peasants didn't understand the intricacies of the law and had nothing with which to bribe the bureaucracy. "We went to Manila back in the 1960s to complain," a peasant said, his eyes bulging. "We went from one senator's office to another. But we ended up being denounced. They said we were *kainginero* and we were wrecking the forest." *Kainginero* practiced slash-and-burn agriculture and were traditionally blamed for forest denudation. A few years back, in an attempt to shore up the economy, Marcos had lifted controls on the export of forest products. The Philippines became the fifth-leading world supplier of hardwood, and it lost nearly all its forests. And still the country failed to produce its own paper. "The damage to peasant land by the run-offs," said Luneta, "is incalculable. Sometimes, an entire harvest would be drowned out by mountain torrents."

The first organizers arrived in 1974; they left after only a few months. Not until 1977 did two more—one with relatives in the area—come to stay. They managed to start a small Party committee composed mostly of clan-kins. According to one peasant, it was the first time within the memory of even the oldest barrio resident that nonpeasants had been interested in how peasants thought or felt or saw the world. The effect of this humanization was fast organizational growth. Since the second line of organizers knew every nook and cranny of the place, it was only a matter of time before "consolidation" was achieved.

As far as I could see, "consolidation" primarily meant an infrastructure that not only managed political, ideological, and organizational work but also administered the whole community on the level of daily, personal problems, ranging from habitual drunkenness to wife beating to putting together work-sharing teams. It also meant having a network that was stable enough to sustain and nurture full-time *mandirigma* ("warriors") whose main concern was to intensify the war of attrition against the government military.

Much of the initial work involved convincing peasants that change was possible. That it was necessary was not debatable. For two weeks, escorted by a squad of six, we threaded through a landscape of poverty. We walked up and down mountain ridges as our fully armed "security" kept an eye out for troop movements and helicopters. They did not seem particularly attentive. Ka Paula (*Ka* was short for *Kasama*, "companion," an old peasant honorific that the underground now used for "comrade"), the designated leader of our group, was confident enough at one point to hand me her baby armalite. "Why don't you carry this for a while?" she asked. I slung the weapon; it was heavy. "What happens if we meet a patrol?" I asked. "Do you know how to use this?" I shook my head. She sighed. "I'd better hold it; if we do meet a patrol, you might start shooting at everything and kill me." She laughed.

That ended my warrior career. I was back to Team Baker. Our group had been divided at the trek's start into three teams: Team Abel was the assault component; it would pin down the enemy. Team Baker was the "protect-ee" group; it had to duck and listen for instructions. Team Charlie was cover; it would draw gunfire away from Team Baker. Instructions were simple. Directions were designated by numbers: six was straight ahead; seven, to the right; eight, to the left; and nine, to the back. Ka Paula would shout out "retreat" or "advance" to the appropriate number. At night as we slept in peasant huts, I could never remember where direction six lay. Ka Paula sighed again and gave me the names of three barrios to hide in and two to avoid in case I got separated.

Whenever we entered a barrio, peasants poured out of their huts and offered "coffee"—made from roasted and ground peanuts—or young coconuts. They apologized for not having ice cubes. One dinnertime caught us near a barrio, and I saw an elderly woman carrying the lone village hen off to the kitchen. I had to lie and say we ate nothing but vegetables. "What kind?" she asked. "Anything," I said. "We have radishes at the *kaingin*,*" she said, looking doubtful. I assured her we loved nothing better than radishes. She released the hen and took off; it was only then that I realized the *kaingin* was a long climb up into the wilderness. But the radishes were good, and in the morning the hen woke us with her cackling.

Our presence was reason enough for the peasants to drop their work and gather. Ka Paula did the introductions. Ka Rowena saw to our accommodations. The others disappeared; I assumed they were reconnoitering. The peasants found a voyager from America irresistible. To them, the United States was still the land of the beautiful, the bountiful, and the mighty. They were taken aback when I said there were poor people in America. "Why can't the poor there hasten their revolution," one asked, "so we can help each other? We will fight here; they can fight there, and together, we can pin down the enemy." I had no answer. "What do Americans think of our movement?" an old man

* small cleared land in the mountain forest; usually planted to rice or vegetables.

who'd lost most of his teeth asked. Hm. How did one explain that although the United States was—had been since 1898—a major force and factor in the Philippines, the reverse was not true? That the Philippines was only one of a hundred small countries that vied for American attention; that the ocean and lack of information—and what little information there was was filtered through Western eyes—made events in the archipelago seem like incomprehensible happenings in a never-never land?

I tried—and they were both disappointed and offended that they were only a pinprick to a people, a country that commanded their own full attention. An old man squatting in front of the crowd shifted his weight. "You're telling us we should not concern ourselves with others, that we should just take care of this, of what's ours, and that we should not expect others to understand or to help?" I hesitated; we were circling moral dilemmas here. Did one dampen their newly awakened humanity and encourage a cynical view of mankind? Or should one give them a beautiful lie to ease the days ahead? From the edge of the crowd, Ka Rowena grinned.

"*Tatang* ('father')," I said, hoping I would be gentle enough, "help and understanding should come on your own terms. What you do and will do shouldn't be in the expectation that others will approve of your actions. No one can understand your situation better than you. No one can resolve your problems better than you." Silence; nods. The group broke up shortly after that. Ka Rowena came up and said "*Nakapasabak ka* ('You walked into that one')." Ka Paula laughed: "*Nag-d.g. si 'mare* ('Our friend conducted a discussion group')." I was less sanguine, sure I had given no hope, no reassurance, and that I had disappointed my countrymen.

Fortunately, the guerrillas interacted with the peasants on a different plane. Our group's three women were trained in acupuncture, and they readily complied with the peasants' request for a *turok* ("injection"). The New People's Army was the sole source of affordable medicine and of rudimentary technology here. Ka Baldo, at forty the oldest of our group, had helped devise the split bamboo tubes that piped in water from a mountain spring. Beyond that, the ubiquitous Coke, Pepsi, and cigarettes were the only artifacts of modern times. Even the public elementary school, which was half a day's walk away, could hold classes only thrice a week; the single teacher doubled up for classes at different levels.

Such poverty was not only heartbreaking; it was also unnecessary. The area produced enough for Eduardo "Danding" Cojuangco, a Marcos crony, to set up a coconut mill in the nearby town. But as in the rest of the rural areas, property relations obstructed progress and development. The landowners, some of whom had obtained ownership through deceit, demanded half the coconut harvest after deducting the rental of tools and the cost of seed nuts and other items that they had provided. "In such issues, the NPA tends to intervene as little as possible," Luneta said. "The peasants are encouraged to deal with the problem themselves. To band together, to organize, and then confront the landowner. If the latter is recalcitrant, then the guerrillas send word that it would be better for everyone if he negotiated with his tenants. Sometimes our presence alone is enough to convince the landlord to sit down with his workers." Of the 212 landlords whom the peasants had contacted, only two had not agreed to a new 70-30 division. "They're still talking," Luneta said, shrugging.

The process of peasant empowerment could be tortuous and slow, and even highly disciplined guerrillas could become impatient. "We had one case where a commander intervened," said Luneta. "The landlord had ordered the bulldozing of his tenants' huts. It was an extreme situation, of course, but even then, the commander was censured. It would've been better if the tenants had acted themselves to stop the bulldozers."

But at the Cojuangco mill, protected as it was by a detachment of the Philippine Constabulary, the guerrillas took direct action. "The mill, the PC camp, and the town hall were hit simultaneously," Luneta said. This was in November 1985, which also saw the emergence of Southern Luzon's First Red Company, headed by Ka Teban. He had been an Armed City Partisan, the NPA's urban-based component, and had had to turn "full time" after dispatching a town mayor with a single shot. He'd been a student at the University of the Philippines' Los Banos agricultural school branch. He looked so familiar, I committed the faux pas of asking whether we had met before. "Probably not," he answered brusquely. Full-time warriors consigned their past to the past, his manner said.

A call for volunteers had been issued, Luneta recalled, and even militia members came asking to be allowed to join the raid. "You'd think it was a fiesta; everybody wanted to be part of it. Even the townspeople," he said, shaking his head. "On the way back, the guerrillas passed through a barrio which had been preparing for a wedding for the following day. When they heard about the raid, the peasants decided to feed the guerrillas and just cook again for the wedding." Plans for the raid were discussed with those who were to participate, and although changes were not allowed in the conduct of the raid itself, warriors and volunteers could ask for a change of assignments. "Or even drop out of it entirely," Luneta said. "You don't hold it against a person if he's not ready. But ask your companions. They were there."

I looked at my escorts with new eyes. Ka Isabel had joined us by accident. She'd been staying at a peasant hut, waiting for her paramedic team to return from their vacation leaves, when we passed by. After learning she was only fifteen years old, I had impulsively asked her to come with us. She had glanced at Ka Paula, and when the latter had nodded, her face had blazed with joy that only the very young are capable of. She had made me glad for her presence when in one peasant's hut I'd innocently asked a boy lying nearby, half covered by a faded blanket, if he was ill. It turned out he'd been gored by a water buffalo that afternoon; all the time we'd been chatting, his blood had been seeping through the bamboo slats to the earth under the house. Isabel had been trained as a paramedic by the guerrillas and she took charge immediately, ferreting among her meager supplies for antibiotics, using acupressure to stop the bleeding. But when she asked the boy's parents for a clean cloth—a T-shirt maybe, which could be ripped—they had shamefacedly confessed that they had nothing, nothing at all.

I thought Isabel must have stood guard at a street corner during the Cojuangco raid, but when I asked what her role had been, she said, "Assault." Ka Winner, nineteen, and Ka Timmy, twenty-four, both so quiet one tended to forget their presence, had also been in assault teams. They were veterans of half a dozen raids, though they had averaged only about two years' service each. But they didn't like talking; being peasant youths, they were shy and diffident. "We rode in trucks," Ka Isabel said, squinting as if she could make me see through her eyes."It's very quiet when you're going to the target. Nobody talks. But afterwards, it's like a party. Everybody kids everybody."

Ka Timmy had broken his left leg when he jumped from the truck. "I didn't notice," he said. "I was thinking I had to provide the covering gunfire because the comrades were pushing ahead. Then the order to move forward came, and my leg refused." He was embarrassed. The assault teams had managed to disable almost all the soldiers; the others ran away. "A raid is very quick, only minutes. You know it's over when you hear the cease-fire order. Then you hear the soldiers' voices calling out 'Surrender! Surrender!' But one sergeant hid himself in the toilet. One of the comrades shoved its door open, and bang! He got it." Luneta explained that although the younger soldiers gave up easily, the older military men tended to fight longer, with more tenacity. When the raid took longer than expected, the young guerrillas would get so excited, they'd take off their combat boots. "We keep telling them not to do that," Luneta said. "We try to issue each one boots, but they complain that they're too heavy; that they can't move quickly enough in those boots. But you know, running through broken glass and everything, they injure themselves." I checked the boots; they were regulation U.S.-designed, Korea-manufactured military footwear.

I asked the three men in our group whether they had been afraid. They shook their heads. "Before you're allowed to go on a raid," Ka Winner said, "the political officers make sure that death is no longer a problem with you, that that question has been resolved." Ka Timmy nodded. "Resolved," he said. "Life and death resolved." How exactly did one resolve that question? They looked at one another, scratched their heads, and frowned. "It does not concern you anymore," Ka Timmy ventured. How could your own death not concern you? They thought for a while and could only come up with the word *lutas* ("solved"). Finally, the exasperated Ka Timmy blurted out, "It means your own death doesn't matter anymore, that you have dedicated your life, and whether you die sooner or later makes no difference." Having brought out this thing he lived by, he turned beet red.

Suffering only two fatalities, they had confiscated firearms, cash, and twenty-five typewriters from the raid, had immobilized the town hall, and had held a two-hour public lecture attended by the townspeople. In the guerrilla printing house—a makeshift hut buried deep in the secondary growth of the wilderness—there was an incongruous office wall clock. "That's Cojuangco's," Ka Paula said, "and we still don't know what to do with the typewriters. Wanna buy one?"

We walked every day, climbing up and going down ravines, our paths crisscrossed by children who brought news of "enemy movements." The NPA was changing not only the politics but also the lifestyle in the area. Many of the boys affected the bullet-pendant necklace that guerrillas wore, as well as Luneta's well-patched pants. "They didn't realize I wasn't being fashionable, that my pants seats were simply worn through," Luneta said. "Now they put patches even on new pants." And everywhere peasants recounted their own "encounters" with the military. "I was cutting grass for our water buffalo," a toothless old woman said, "when a patrol came. I was ready to go home, but I thought I should try to see where they were going. Then the sergeant drew up; he was at the end of the line. He looked at me and said, 'Well, have you finished counting us?'" She laughed.

Despite their "resolution" of the life-and-death question, the guerrillas remained intensely aware of the perilous nature of their existence. One manifestation of this was an incurable romanticism. A stranger was asked often and obliquely whether she was married, pledged to someone, or available. It was light banter, of course. Strict rules governed personal relations among the people of the underground, partly in response to peasant culture. Courtship and marriage happened only upon the consent of the collectives to which the couple belonged. It was preferable that a couple be at the same level of ideological development; if not, the more "advanced" partner had the responsibility of uplifting the other. Pre- and extramarital sex were not acceptable.

Ka Rowena had briefed me how to conduct myself. "Blouses buttoned up to here," she said, gesturing at my neck, "even in summertime. And no bathing in underwear or in the nude. If a peasant sees you, he's likely to be scared out of his wits." But within the constraints of peasant tradition, the NPA did institute profound changes. Both men and women had the right to initiate courtship. "Some of my women friends have done that," Isabel said. "A few won; a few were disappointed." How did women cope with rejection, considering how much they had to overcome psychologically to court men? "You sit down with the political officer," she said, "or a friend or a co-member of the collective. You analyze what happened, where you drew the wrong conclusions, or where you and the man didn't match. No, nobody thinks it's a shameful thing." But she acknowledged that it still hurt no matter what. "However, you can try again," she added brightly.

The key to the success of these initial efforts at gender

equality was the women's association, one of three organizations that formed the village collective life. The other two were the youth and peasant associations; the latter were joined largely by family heads—i.e., adult males. Embedded within the three were Party cadres who had their own smaller collectives. But it was the women who were most aggressive about doing war work; they enjoyed intelligence and reconnaisance missions. They liked walking into a military camp, bearding the lion in his den, as it were, going as cooked-food vendors, laundry women, and odd jobbers for soldiers. In the process, they memorized the camp layout, counted military personnel, and learned the camp routine. It was rather disconcerting to hear all this discussed by a dozen women—some gray-haired, most missing teeth, their bodies misshapen, babies tugging at their withered breasts—huddled in a hut in the middle of nowhere.

They were aware, of course, that it was no game. The peasants remember a colleague who had run out of his hut to save some chickens during a flood. A military patrol spotted him and gunned him down without warning. And many had been roughed up, their food supply and property confiscated. Still, there were compensations. "Three barrios from here," a peasant said, "the lands were titled, and those who'd created the coconut farms were driven out. God knows it would've happened here as well, if not for the presence of the guerrillas."

Beyond affirming the value and rightness of the peasants' existence, the New People's Army also represented a singular opportunity of escape from the semisentience of rural life. Ka Baldo said he had been a farmer all his life. "But every year, at harvest time, when I summed up my work, I was always at the losing end. I thought to myself, What the hell kind of life is this? I couldn't make even a single step forward. *Talo, talo* ('defeated'). By chance, a squad came through my fields. I wasn't married; I had no family. *Jala!* I just up and went with them. I didn't even think. I knew nothing about politics or whatnot. I learned along the way. I just didn't care." Since then, he'd been to places he'd never dreamed of reaching, like the Montañosa, the mountain-range home of tribal Filipinos.

I understood then why the village youth looked at the guerrillas with such envy. They had "made it": they were adequately fed, clothed, and trained; and through the guerrilla network, they were linked with what was going on in the rest of the world. On the other hand, whenever peasants gathered, one could see their past, present, and future laid out—exact, unchanging. One could see it in the children, bird-boned and stunted, as lethargic as the village dog that came to sniff without enthusiasm at visitors' legs; in the brief flowering of the teenagers; in the abrupt darkness of parents still in their thirties but already misshapen by labor and childbearing; and in the final withering of fifty-year-old grandparents plagued by aches and pains. Peasants were born quickly, matured early, and died young, their passing as unremarked as the trees and cogon grass of their habitation.

No wonder Ka Isabel folded and refolded the contents of her knapsack—her shirts, her pants, her medical kit, a plastic reed mat—with care. These, along with her ammo vest and her carbine, were the demarcations of her being. They lifted her from the stultifying anonymity of the poverty around her. It was clear that neither she nor the rest of the "gang"—including the even-younger Raymond, and a twelve-year-old boy who'd been with the guerrillas since he was eight, and the still unmarried Ka Baldo—would even think of abandoning their truly dangerous but adventurous existence.

"As you can see," Luneta said, "at the core of the revolution is the land question. Agrarian revolution fuels the entire movement in the countryside. Marcos is merely an issue, one of the factors which exacerbate the land problem. He is not *the* reason for the revolution."

FIVE

Things Past and Present

When he and his friends began setting up the underground, Jose Luneta said, they told one another they'd be lucky to live beyond the age of thirty. "The only solution was to build a mass movement. This meant extensive and widespread education, fast recruitment, and relentless organizing. We kept 'elevating' activists into cadres and more cadres. Each time one fell, at least five had to be ready to take his place." Since the peasantry was the one inexhaustible source of manpower, it was logical that organizing should concentrate on this sector. In 1970, anticipating a political crisis, the underground core seeded the archipelago with volunteer students, intellectuals, and déclassé activists from Manila to a dozen regions. The toll on this first line of organizers was terrible. Following the declaration of martial law, when the military was no longer held back by legal constraints, the average lifespan of a rural cadre was reduced to one year at best. He was immobilized by imprisonment, injuries, or death. Even in Manila, the germinal National Democratic Front, which was working to build a coalition of middle, church, and revolutionary forces, lost three levels of leadership in as many years. Nevertheless, replacements were found; the underground steadily gained legitimacy as the only organized and large-scale opposition to the Marcos regime. In the course of this indefatigable work in areas where the regime's control was weak, the underground also transformed itself from an intellectual-led political "tempest in a teapot" to a peasant-based revolution.

This would not have been possible if dreamer-poet Jose Ma. Sison had not met Bernabe Buscayno, aka Commander Dante, an equally young peasant who'd ripened with the remnants of the old Hukbong Mapagpalaya ng Bayan (HMB, or People's Liberation Army). The HMB had led the Central Luzon guerrilla resistance against the Japanese invasion in World War II, as well as the 1950s Huk rebellion. But by the 1960s, it had deteriorated into an army-for-hire band, used for protection rackets and to ensure the victory of rich politicians.

"Fate must've been reserving me for something," Sison recalled. "Sumulong [then HMB head] sent word twice that he wanted to meet me. The first time I could not make it; the second time, I got to the rendezvous place an hour late. If we had met, he would have had me killed. Undoubtedly." Young HMB commanders who disagreed with Sumulong's policies disappeared or were ambushed.

Sison had not known about Buscayno. But the latter's curiosity had been pricked by reports about the cantankerous KM. He was already disaffected with the HMB, which had become more of a business operation than a political movement. Since he moved in Tarlac, Buscayno turned to some Aquino associates and asked that a meeting with the "professor" [Sison] be arranged. Shortly thereafter, the Party was established; three months later, the New People's Army was born. The two men would be acknowledged to be the founders of both.

"It was in Barrio Sta. Rita, Tarlac," recounted a teacher

who had been present at the NPA's founding. "We had been there for around two weeks, preparing documents, giving lectures. A house had been built for us at the edge of the village—bigger than the ordinary hut. There were about ten of us Manila intellectuals. We did not realize how noticeable our presence was. We were so amateurish. Ours was the only house lit up with Coleman lamps. And there were too many people coming and going and staying. Then one woman in the group had this big transistor radio, and she liked tuning in to Radio Beijing every night at ten o'clock. Full blast. It's a wonder we weren't all wiped out." The defecting HMB guerrillas, seasoned in the ways of war, had been uneasy for days. "But—well, they were peasants," the teacher said, "very diffident. They couldn't warn us. Finally a commander came, and his men told him. But even he would speak only to my wife, because she spoke his native language. When we learned about it, we were so mortified."

On March 29, 1969, the actual plenum of establishment was held. "The commanders started arriving with their squad escorts. Now they say there were thirty-five rifles and sixty men. My impression then was there were more." He began ticking off names on his fingers: Commander Melody, Pusa, and more. Most had fallen by the wayside. "But we were all waiting for Dante," he said, smiling. "He was legendary even then. Finally, two men arrived; one, tall, handsome, big, with a lantern jaw; the other, small, thin, wimp-looking. I eyed the big guy who radiated confidence. So, I thought, that's how Dante looks. No wonder he's so famous. The tall guy remained standing, while the thin one took a chair, sat with his feet on the seat edge and his chin on his knees. He kept laughing and covering his mouth shyly each time he laughed.

"Well, you guessed it. The small guy was Dante; the other, his bodyguard. Shows you how much intellectuals know." He scratched his head. "So we were gathered, and everyone went through the documents sentence by sentence. At the end of it, someone announced that the New

People's Army was now in operation, and everybody clapped. For me, it was anticlimactic. Dante disappointed me. He looked so ordinary."

But Dante, whose life history was unknown and whose only available photograph was taken when he was seventeen years old, gave the underground the legend of the simple and saintly peasant forced to take up arms against his fate. To Manila oppositionists who never met him, he was the knight in shining armor who would someday ride into the city from the vastness of the countryside to end Marcos's power. During the mid-1970s "conflagration"— waves of arrests and seizures, in activist lingo—I found myself paralyzed in the Cubao shopping district when a newsboy thrust a Marcos paper under my nose. DANTE CAPTURED, said the banner headline. Never before nor since had the regime seemed so powerful, so fully in control, as in that instant. On television, Marcos paraded all the "legendary names" he held in his prisons: Victor Corpuz, Jose Luneta, Saturnino Ocampo, beauty queen Nelia Sancho, and others. Silent and feeling sicker every minute, a dozen of us Manila intellectuals watched the television show at a rich friend's home. At the end of it, our hostess, presiding over an ornate silver coffee and tea service, peered into our faces and said, "But it will go on, won't it? It's not the end, is it?"

Only two members of the KT-KS (Executive Committee of the Central Committee) survived that conflagration. "They had to call on the heads of the regional commissions to come forth and identify themselves," Luneta said. "They didn't know one another. But the good thing about the leadership which formed in 1977 was that they came from different regions. They had a truly national character. The first leaders had an understanding of the national situation on an overall scale; they worked out the general directions for the development of the revolution. But the second leadership had the practical knowledge to implement and refine those directions." Luneta himself had not been worried by the mid-1970s arrests. "We knew the movement was over the hump by 1974. The nucleus of ten regional commissions had been set up. And also, both *The Specific Characteristics of Our People's War* and *Our Urgent Tasks* had been written." Authored by Amado Guerrero, these set down the strategy and tactics of the revolution. It was indicative of the intellectual origins of the underground that the resolution of a problem in thought was as important as its resolution in reality.

It took about two years to rebuild the underground infrastructure. By 1979, the New People's Army was well into its geometric expansion, while the National Democratic Front had stabilized and could drop the phrase "preparatory commission" from its name. In 1980, there were ten thousand full-time guerrillas. Simultaneously, the failure of Marcos's export-oriented and foreign capital–led economic program began to manifest itself. The currency was taking its first tentative devaluation; it would become a rapid slide within the next four years. By this time, the military was accusing Rodolfo Salas of being the new underground leader, and he was being described as power hungry, ruthless, and war oriented. I couldn't quite see the shy, always smiling, mere slip of a boy I had known that way.

When I met him again, I scrutinized him carefully, probing for his alleged cold bloodedness and ruthlessness. He had been a student at the University College of Engineering and had not been as quarrelsome as the humanities component of our "gang." He had been a steady worker, silent at his tasks—from mimeographing statements about this or that issue to buying bottles of Coke for our midafternoon snack. Because he was never as vocal as the others, my memories of him were vivid and yet indefinite. I could tell his wife, though, that he was probably the only one in our group with whom I hadn't had a fight. His wife smiled. "That's also what he said," she said.

While I was tracking him down, a number of people had told me stories about him: that he'd shown up unexpectedly at a friend's house; that he looked worn out and exhausted and had taken aspirin; that he'd fallen asleep and awakened three hours later, as if by an internally determined alarm;

that he looked so unprepossessing, he would attend meetings and mass assemblies in Manila unnoticed. He surprised his wife once by apologizing for not having paid her enough attention through the years, for having been unable to take her out on a "date."

Now he was here with his round granny eyeglasses, which had given him his nickname, Bilog ("circle"). He was unarmed, with no bodyguards—only his wife and son. He had barely aged; he'd only filled out, so he was lean and wiry. He had the economy of movement of the confident and was certainly more articulate. Although he would neither confirm nor deny the allegations against him, he agreed to answer my questions to the best of his knowledge.

Corazon C. Aquino's candidacy was problematic for the Left. Although she was definitely an "antifascist" personality, her lack of a political track record made judgment difficult. On the one hand, she came from the traditional ruling class of the country; the Aquino sugar plantation, the Hacienda Luisita, was run like a classic feudal fiefdom. On the other hand, some activists who had been thrown into contact with her during her husband's incarceration and trial (with Bernabe Buscayno and Victor Corpuz, he received the death sentence from a military tribunal) reported having had "good" experiences with her.

But apart from judging her character, the Left was also faced with the challenge of judging the entire electoral practice in general and the 1986 presidential election in particular. "The country has had elections since 1946," Salas said, "and beyond that, in the 1930s, when the Commonwealth government was set up. We have been asked to choose mostly between candidates coming from factions and wings of the economically privileged. The basic question was whether elections were a significant exercise in themselves within the current sociopolitical system, whether they could create a government which would hold primary the interests of the majority, of the workers and peasants, against those of a powerful splinter of the population." He lighted a Marlboro, exhaled, and suddenly smiled.

"You know the answer to that one—by experience and by history. Marcos was a child of our political system."

He himself did not feel that the Left should encourage the people in false hopes. Instead of allowing themselves to be "trapped" within a process predetermined by the ruling class, he thought the people should look beyond what was being made available, perhaps to other forms of democratic process. Also, overt U.S. pressure on the Marcos regime to hold the election indicated that the whole procedure would be not only beyond the control of the majority, but also not totally within national control.

Nevertheless, when the underground first met to discuss the possibility of a snap election, "the leaders did consider the popular response to it," Salas said. "The first decision was to participate—but only if certain conditions were met. Those conditions would have raised the quality of the electoral process. Without them, the ballot would have been simply a negative vote—one against the regime, not *for* anything else. It would have meant a return to personality politics, something no better than a popularity or beauty contest. We've had those for decades."

The underground wanted the inclusion in the candidates' programs of certain principles that it felt were necessary to the nation's economic well-being and its sovereignty. "Everybody was sure Marcos would cheat," Salas said, "and there was no way of preventing him from doing so, nor of correcting the fraud he would inflict on the nation—at least, not within the existing constitutional framework. He controlled the state, the institutions which would decide who the winner was. For the election to become more than just an exercise in futility, fundamental issues—not just whether this candidate was better than the other—had to be the crux of the debate. When that did not materialize—Mrs. Aquino, though preferable as an individual to the dictator, did not present any program of government—the Left swung to its other alternative: to boycott the election as this was defined by the two political parties. And to set its own parameters of participation. Instead of endorsing a specific candidate—which would have been dangerous for the candidate, anyway—it chose to raise the question of whether elections held within a dictatorship were a viable democratic process. Never forget that Marcos was ousted by extralegal action, not through the election."

The KT-KS met in December 1985, and the debate was long and intense. According to Jose Luneta, the boycott call won by the narrowest of margins; someone else told me that it had been a three-two split. In midmonth, the KT-KS issued its now-famous "boycott memorandum." To Salas, the key phrase in the memo was "all Party-led organizations." The Communist Party, the New People's Army, and other banned organizations of the National Democratic Front really had no alternative except to boycott. They existed outside the constitutional framework, since mere membership in the Party and organizations deemed "Communistic" was punishable by death. But for some time now, the Left had been—and still was—the sole organizing force of the anti-Marcos resistance. Its cadres, sympathizers, and allies—men and women who in varying degrees respected the underground—were present in almost all the major opposition groups. They were either leaders or workhorses in these organizations and when they opted for a boycott, all hell broke loose. Arguments and debates erupted; personal enmities were created.

"The peasantry had little difficulty with the boycott," Salas said. And indeed, in the zone I visited some peasants had walked for two days to join boycott rallies in the town proper. Nor did the workers seem to have any difficulty with the concept. The country's largest labor union, the Kilusang Mayo Uno, voted to boycott ahead of everyone else, with some unionists joking later that even the KT-KS followed their lead. "But in the urban areas and towns, among the middle class and the elite oppositionists—that was where all the furor came from," Salas said.

Many of the five hundred or so cause-oriented organizations (ranging in size from those with a few hundred members to large, nationwide coalitions with tens of thousands of members) that arose during the martial law years voted to boycott, in recognition of the points raised by the KT-KS memo against the election. But many did so with a heavy heart, knowing that the stand, though principled, would anger many middle-class and rich allies. "You have no idea," said a feminist organizer, "how difficult it was to get the comfortable to accept the idea of fighting an established authority. Next, you had to convince them it was possible to fight the regime at least to a stalemate. Then they had to get used to the idea that their vote in an organization had only equal weight as the votes of those who were poorer, couldn't speak English, and wore thong rubber slippers to meetings. Somehow, I don't think we were very successful with the last one. The rich, after all, had been ordering the poor about far longer than they'd been listening to them." She laughed.

Though the question of whether to boycott or to participate was submitted to a vote of the general membership, some of the middle-class and elite members equated the rejection of their political stand with a personal rejection. They abandoned the organizations and joined the campaign. Others preferred to avoid the problem by taking leaves of absence, while many more, including cadres and organizers who disagreed with the KT-KS memo, chose to involve themselves in "poll watchdog" organizations like NAMFREL, TAPAT, and so on.

"I do not think there was pressure to get a boycott decision where one wasn't possible," said Salas. "From the KT-KS, none that I know of. But some overzealous organizers may have tried to force the decision in their own groups." On the other hand, some of the "middle forces," their desire for a collective kick at Marcos's face frustrated, simply shut their doors and refused to have anything to do with the great unwashed thereafter.

What happened, said one political science professor, was a manifestation of the "chasm" between the upper 20 percent of the population and the lower 80 percent. "Let's face it," he said, "were it not for the pervasive oppressive character of the Marcos regime, the two population segments would have been totally different countries. Different needs, different interests, different visions for the future; different cultures and different languages, even. The only reason the 20 percent considered working with the poor was, the Aquino assassination scared them shitless. They found themselves suddenly vulnerable. *Good grief, Marcos could kill us and the United States won't do anything!* They started groping around for allies.

"Then, when they could show that the poor would mobilize behind them, they started talking to Washington. When it became clear they could remove Marcos without incurring the wrath of the United States, it also became clear that they would not have to make concessions to the poor." He made a face. "Historically, this nation has always been betrayed by its upper class—because they think they are the nation. *L'etat c'est moi.* Why shouldn't you boycott if you were poor? Mrs. Aquino offered nothing. What does the 80 percent need? The peasants need land; the workers need fair wages and acceptable working conditions; the middle class need relief from the horrible policies of the International Monetary Fund; the small businessmen need guarantees that their businesses won't be subject to monopoly takeovers and unfair competition from foreign capital; the urban poor need housing; and I can't even begin to tell you what the women need. Reduce that to basics—food, clothing, shelter, education, meaningful work, the opportunity to make something out of yourself, not just be a talking animal. Reduce that to something even more basic: to be in control, even in minimal control, of forces shaping your existence. Excuse me, but I boycotted. I decided back in 1972 I would boycott every election that didn't even offer a glimmer of this. Besides which, Mrs. Aquino did make clear she didn't want to work with the cause-oriented groups."

But a leftist intellectual disagreed. The problem was, he said, that the KT-KS first failed to see that an insurrectionary situation obtained in the urban areas; then second, it formulated its decision based on abstract principles, not on the specifics of the situation it faced; and third, it made no provisions for action after the election—despite its own anticipation that Marcos would cheat on a massive scale. "If you looked at it coldbloodedly," he said, "the Left dug a semantical trap for itself. If they had called the decision 'critical participation' and done exactly what they did during the campaign and the election—which was to hold mass assemblies, marches, seminars, and forums around the election issue—the elite opposition would have been unable to belittle the Left's contribution. If organized labor had issued a general strike threat should Marcos cheat, then—well, we could go into a lot of ifs."

Salas said the underground believed that the United States would not risk "destabilizing" Marcos, that he would be allowed to remain in power until 1987, when his term expired. This conclusion was based on the 1985 U.S. National Security Study Document "U.S. Policy Towards the Philippines." Rather than seeing the document as a reflection of the U.S. government's growing worry about the Philippine situation, the KT-KS interpreted it as a vote of confidence for Marcos. It was strange that the underground, which assumed that the U.S. government had the power to maintain the regime despite national opposition, did not consider the possibility that it could also have the power to remove him at any time. Even stranger was its reliance on a document released by what the Left called the "puppetmaster" of all Philippine governments.

According to National Democratic Front spokesman Antonio Zumel, there had been no indication at all that the United States would agree to Marcos's removal. Aid was continuing, the International Monetary Fund was still trying to shore up the economy with loans, and arms shipments were pouring in. "But there were a number of things wrong with the KT-KS decision," he said. "I'm not a member of that body, but it has been pointed out that the KT-KS was too small a base for a decision of such scope and importance. Perhaps the Central Committee itself should have taken it up—though that, too, would not be large enough to be democratically representative."

Zumel, a former president of the National Press Club, had gone underground in 1972 upon the declaration of martial law. Slightly older than the activists who idolized him at the time, Zumel was the particular "legend" of print media people. Before martial law, he had turned the offices of the National Press Club—which was near Congress—into a sanctuary for demonstrators chased by the police. I was so used to his being Club president that when I went to see the current one, I asked two cigarette boys in the parking lot where "Zumel's office" was. The two looked at each other; then the younger kid lifted his eyes to the horizon and said, "Zumel? *Nakuu* ('Oh, dear'). He's been gone a *looong* time. He went to the boondocks." Zumel cracked up when I told him about the incident. It must have been flattering to be known even by those born after one had become a nonperson to the society.

In the bitter aftermath of the boycott debate, some cadres "violated discipline" and began publicly circulating documents critical of the KT-KS and crying for the heads of those who had made the decision. Also, internal Party documents were leaked to the media, and security arrangements were broken. A few members defected to small, rival leftist groups and denounced the NDF. At some point, personal letters for underground members were blocked during transmission from Manila. Zumel shook his head. "Even comrades can be harsh," he said. "The bitterness is understandable." Part of it came from the misconception that the revolution could have been won right there and then, if only the KT-KS had made the right decision. "Even we believe that the New People's Army won't be the only army of the revolution," Zumel said. "We expect others to arise, and while the NPA will function as the core of this new national army, [the latter] will be made up of many armies, many forces. We have offered our Moslem brothers equal partnership, for instance. We have proposed forming a still higher coalition where the NDF will only be one component."

Salas himself was surprised by the "misconception" that the NPA could have taken Manila. "I don't think they have that capability yet," he said. He had long been bemused by Western press reports about the strength of the "insurgency." A 20,000-member resistance force was certainly no match for the 250,000-member armed forces of the Philippines, supplied directly by the United States. Still, the strength of the Left's *political* influence was undeniable. The National Democratic Front could claim control of 20 to 25 percent of all provincial barrios.

Nonetheless, this was not yet a formula for victory. Moving the struggle from the stage of "strategic stalemate" to "strategic offensive," Luneta explained, entailed a quantum jump. "So far, we haven't found the key," he said. It wasn't the guerrillas' fault. Day and night, at every possible minute, the warriors did nothing but look for a chance to hit the enemy and amass weapons. "Relentless," Luneta said. "We've had tactical offensives almost daily. Tracking down the soldiers, looking for an opening."

War technology posed the greatest problem. A member of the Mindanao underground confirmed that only the lack of hardware was holding back the guerrillas. "Bear in mind, we face a brutal military supplied by the United States," she said. "That means the most advanced weaponry." The NDF received little help from overseas; it remained a homegrown and self-reliant revolution. I asked Salas about rumors of overtures from the Soviet Union. He shook his head. "I believe that was turned down," he said, "because Russia would not repudiate the old CP." The latter had surrendered to Marcos in 1974, and many of its leaders now worked within the regime's bureaucracy.

The woman from Mindanao recounted that in their area the military had abruptly raised the technological level of warfare. "It took us two years to match it," she said, "and as soon as we did, they raised it again. Now, with these heligunships from the U.S., I don't know. We'll have to think of something else. Are surface-to-air-missiles on sale in Manhattan department stores?" She laughed.

But levity aside, both she and Salas pointed out that the very mass nature of the movement brought its own problems. The underground, Salas explained, had investigated reports of NPA atrocities and had discovered that they were committed by military operatives disguised as guerrillas, if they were not actually part of guerrilla units. "The existence of Oplan Cadena-de-Amor [a military counter-insurgency tactic] would not have been discovered," he said, "if one of the 'zombies' [agents and spies] had not been conscience-stricken and confessed." What happened was that the military had extrapolated the general direction of guerrilla expansion and had dropped its operatives in adjoining barrios, where they had set up a peasant existence. When a guerrilla squad came and asked for volunteers, the "zombies" joined. "In Mindanao, I understand that at one point the guerrillas had close to about fifty 'zombies' under house arrest," Salas said.

My Mindanao friend confirmed this. "In Cagayan de Oro," she said, "the underground was hit six times. None of the leaders lasted more than a month. We realized someone was feeding the military." That was par for the course; the underground had its own intelligence units within the military. "What's not acceptable is the damage they inflict on the civilians, the peasants. Whether done in our name or their name, that's not—well, not nice," she said, punning on the NPA's other common name: Nice People Around. A recent tactic, Luneta said, was to send out operatives disguised as city squatters evicted from their homes. "They build their huts in a barrio and sniff around. But since they have to earn their keep, they report nonsense even when there's nothing to report. Then the patrols come and terrorize the village."

I was told that as a result of the boycott error, the KT-KS chairman and the general secretary accepted responsibility and criticized themselves. The former took a "leave of absence" from his position, though retaining KT-KS membership; the latter resigned. I asked a young man working for the underground military commission about this. He shook his head. "I don't know if Salas was really the chairman," he said, "but if he was—well, you have to give him credit. Based on what I'd heard about the chairman's solid backing from the NPA warriors, he could have suppressed the dissidence militarily. Look at it this way: have you ever heard of a *government* official here admitting error, apologizing, and resigning?" But to use the NPA to suppress dissent, said Salas when I asked him, would have been unprincipled and would have split the revolutionary movement wide open. "We're older and more mature now," he said, and abruptly grinned. "But if this had happened when we were students—*nag-upakan na* ('there would have been full-scale trouble')!"

Zumel would only reply that some comrades, especially those in the urban areas, had no idea of what the leadership they were attacking had gone through. "They don't know," he said, "what difficulties this second leadership took on back in 1976. When no one was around to accept the responsibility of keeping the resistance intact, these men and women stepped forward. And at the time when to obtain even a single sheet of paper for the revolution meant going through incredible hardship." To raise the political consciousness of peasants to the level where they could see themselves in relation to the entire society, one had to begin with the most basic steps—teaching them how to read and write. So a literacy campaign was launched along with the ideological, political, and organizational work.

Salas was inclined to take the hue and cry as merely part of the eternal debate on the strategy and tactics of revolution. "That goes way back to the 1960s," he said. "Not only a discussion of methods but also of what direction this nation should take. You know what that means. You have an entire range of opinions. From the advocates of very slow base-building strategy to the advocates of quick, urban insurrection. From the Chinese model to the Nicaraguan model. And various combinations thereof." He thought this was healthy—healthier certainly than accepting ready-made solutions offered by external agencies and former colonial masters. "We face a very tricky situation," he said. "And I'm not only speaking of the underground but of the entire nation."

Since then, Salas has been arrested by the Aquino government. Zumel has surfaced in Manila as a member of the NDF's panel negotiating with the Aquino government. Luneta, still afflicted with prison phobia, continues to avoid towns and cities. That we had known one another at an earlier stage of our lives undoubtedly affected my interaction with the underground leaders. My familiarity with their premises and assumptions, as well as with small details of the movement's evolution, allowed them to be both more open and more concise in their explanations to me. Also, the very language we used colored the exchange. Luneta and I fell readily into calling each other "boss-chief"—old slang of familiarity and affection; Zumel lapsed into the (mortifyingly ancient) Filipino journalists' term of endearment *mahal* ("beloved"), while with the Salases, it was 'mare and 'pare (literally, one's child's godmother and godfather). Somewhere in the back of my mind, of course, was the feeling that I should be more circumspect. I was, after all, in the presence of men and women who had built, had nurtured, and were now leading a revolution disturbing to the peace of mind of even the mighty U.S. government. On the other hand, our use of the slang of our youth enabled them to show me aspects of their personalities not normally available to strangers.

I could not see them solely in the context of labels. In all probability, all were members of the Communist Party. But like a guerrilla zone, an organization was merely people. I did not doubt that, in the course of their underground lives, they must have had moments of harshness. But I remembered my own blind rage when I heard about how Antonio Hilario had been killed in Aklan. If it had been possible, I would have slit the throat of the first soldier I came upon. Since then, of course, such stories had accumulated, and those stories were the subtext of my conversations with the guerrilla leaders.

They were open about the grief that life in the resistance had brought them. Luneta spoke of the self-doubts he had felt as he lay manacled to his cot in prison; his body had ached from the beatings, the electric shocks, and the burnings. "I wasn't sure I had the capacity to endure," he said. "There was one terrible moment when Col. Miguel Aure came into the room and asked, without preamble, 'Whom do you love more—Sison or your brothers?' They'd been asking me for Sison's whereabouts. I couldn't answer for a while. Then I said, 'Colonel, there's nothing more important than what I believe in, nothing more important than what I'm fighting for. You may kill me, kill my brothers, kill everyone, but ten, twenty years from now, we will rise again.' He stomped out of the room, and I was sure my brothers were dead, that my reply killed them."

Salas, more self-contained, allowed only a moment of revelation. "If the movement had split . . ." he said, referring to the boycott troubles. He couldn't go on. After a while, he said simply, "*Sayang naman* ('It would have been too bad'). One had taken care of it, after all, for almost all of one's life. It's been a long time."

SIX

"There are no elections in this country without cheating," said Arturo Tolentino, a veteran of elections since 1949, a former senator, member of parliament, and foreign affairs minister; he was Ferdinand E. Marcos's running mate in the 1986 snap election. He had been handpicked by the President himself. "I made it clear we might not make a good team," Tolentino recounted, "because I had been critical of some of his policies." But Marcos, saying he wasn't sure how long he would stay on as president, told Tolentino, "Perhaps I will let you go on as president after a couple of years." Tolentino then expected "to be running the government within three years."

He had to be practical. "On my own, I knew I would not make it," he explained. "I had no money. I could never run for the presidency. The only way was through the back door." In 1985 the opposition had made him an offer, but that was before Mrs. Aquino became a candidate. "Besides which, the assemblyman who spoke to me wanted me to sign an impeach-Marcos resolution at the National Assembly without my having read it nor having seen their evidence." He turned it down. Yet another time, he was offered 15 million pesos to run as president. "That would have lasted one week," he said. "I knew Malacanang Palace was going to spend a lot of money." But things did not turn out the way Tolentino, always the odd man out, had expected.

Accustomed to a vigorous campaign, he found the 1986 Marcos roadshow a disappointment. "Mr. Marcos could not go to many places—either because of his health or his schedule or for security reasons. And they would not let me go on my own because that would confirm rumors about his failing health. Even the money—I don't know what happened. I was given very little money. Someone told me the Palace was sure I was going to win anyway, so they didn't think I needed to have much money at my disposal. Later, I learned they gave more to some opposition leaders whom they paid to keep quiet."

He had "great difficulties with the campaign—not physically but with my speeches." He could neither criticize nor defend Marcos, nor "could I talk about our agreement." Still, he had little fear of losing; he hadn't lost an election in his entire life, and he was a favorite even of that bastion of opposition, Metro-Manila. "But I'm sure I was cheated heavily in Southern Tagalog, especially in Batangas, which was Laurel's bailiwick."

Election Day—February 7—was hot, humid, and cloudless. In a small barrio in Bulacan, the outer perimeter of Metro-Manila, the steady *put put put* of motorized pedicabs rent the morning silence as voters hied off to makeshift voting precincts in schoolhouses, lean-tos, and chapels. The man from the Kilusang Bagong Lipunan (KBL)—Marcos's political party—here, the *barangay* ('village') captain, made his rounds in dark depression. Marcos was going to lose, that much was evident; all around and inescapable were the results of the regime's mismanagement. To the north of Bulacan, toward Navotas, Mrs. Marcos had built her Dagat-

dagatan project to reclaim land from the sea; it blocked the egress of river water and high tide. As a result, this little barrio was now coated perpetually by ankle-deep slime; it had once been prime rice land. When Mrs. Marcos started her project, it had seemed possible to turn it into a residential area, so the farmers could recoup their losses. Now it was a quilt of useless rice paddies flooded with water and one or two concrete bungalows whose plumbing was corroded by salt water. A melancholic fishpen or two rose from the water; bamboo slats disturbed the placidity of the rainbow-slick surface. A pair of rubber boots, indispensable equipment now, was slung upended on the rusting spears of an iron fence. The former peasants, waiting for their turn to vote, glared at the eternal flood. They did not relish becoming fishermen.

It was what Adrian Cristobal had called "the bitterness of twenty years." The *barangay* captain grew even more morose when two boys bearing claw hammers came and gestured at the huge Marcos-Tolentino billboard; they asked if they could take it down to patch their house roof with. "Wait until the polls close," he said, "at least." There was no preventing it, he muttered. Marcos was going to lose.

Because everyone knew everyone here, neither terrorism nor cheating was possible—at least not at this stage of the election procedure. The village simply did not have the population density that allowed gunmen to materialize, sweep down on precincts, and disappear again, as they did in some parts of Manila. And because Bulacan wasn't far from the city proper, it was easy to follow the procedure from voting to counting. Still, there were irregularities. One precinct had to delay opening for two hours until the flood waters receded enough to allow the construction of a booth. People also had to scramble from precinct to precinct searching for their names. Though they had registered, they could not find their names listed anywhere. "My husband's name was there," said a middle-aged peddler of cooked food, "even though he didn't vote in 1984. Mine wasn't. I spent the whole morning looking. I'm going back after lunch. Oh, yes, my husband voted for Ronald Reagan." She laughed.

From the neighborhood houses, radios blared out a song by popular folk singer Freddie Aguilar: *I'll find me a millionaire to marry; spend my life traipsing to London, Paris, and New York....* The voting process was tedious, even interminable. For a country claiming to have practiced democracy regularly since 1946, the election procedure was primitive, labor-intensive, and open to intervention at every stage. First one located the precinct where one was listed; then one identified oneself, signed three sheets of documents, accepted a ballot, wrote in the candidates' names, folded it, and dropped it into a ballot box with three padlocks; then one's thumbnail was painted with indelible purple ink. "You pig!" one woman shrieked as a poll official held out a tiny purple-tinged brush. "I just polished my nails!" The ink supposedly marked a person so he or she could not vote again, but acetone removed it easily.

The precincts closed at 5:00 P.M., and the counting was done in public. In a tiny chapel, portable blackboards temporarily hid the icons of the Virgin Mary and Jesus Christ. Tensely, names were read off the ballots, chalk marks were made on the blackboard, and numbers were tallied. In this relatively "clean" precinct, the voting went two to one for Mrs. Aquino; Laurel won by a hair's breadth while the crowd cheered a lone vote that went to a third unknown vice-presidential candidate.

Elsewhere, the improbable was happening. By 7:00 P.M., precincts in the Ilocos region, controlled by Marcos's warlords, were reporting election returns of thirteen thousand for Marcos, zero for Aquino. Asked about this statistical improbability, an Ilocano political leader grinned on television and said, "That is how much we love him." Another, queried as to what had happened to the vote of an Aquino pollwatcher, shrugged and said that perhaps he had been convinced at the last minute to vote for Marcos.

Gunmen swooped down on the Cecilio Apostol Elementary School and closed the precincts. In Balara, Quezon City, thirty-nine-year-old Salvacion Bueno was Aquino's pollwatcher at Precinct 177. At the close of Election Day, some men arrived to take the ballot box to City Hall for counting. Throughout the campaign Salvador Laurel had emphasized the possibility of ballot box switching during transit: "Guard the ballot box," he'd said, "don't let it out of your sight. Defend the ballot box. Bring pieces of wood, anything you can use as clubs." Bueno took the injunction literally and refused to allow anyone else to transport the ballot box. "Men grabbed the box from me," she said, "they said they would take it to City Hall. I refused. I was shoved, pushed, but I would not let go. You can't believe all the trouble I went through. Finally, I sat down on the ballot box and refused to budge. So I myself brought the box to City Hall. Then the Aquino people came to say we had to stand guard at City Hall. So we—my neighbors and friends— went to City Hall and stayed the whole night. After that, we were asked to move to the parliament building, which was so far away, and to mount a vigil there. Off I went again, leaving my seven children."

She took the whole electoral process seriously, she said, because she wanted her children and grandchildren "to taste this thing they call true freedom. To be free to work for a good future for our children. I don't think I've ever had that." She had already spent a month campaigning for Mrs. Aquino, not that she knew the woman. "The poor are the easiest people to ask help from," she said, sighing, "and they're also the easiest to forget once the need for their help is over."

In the island of Cebu, some members of the Washington observer team were blocked from entering a voting precinct in a warlord area. In Guadalupe, Makati, pollwatchers were beaten up. In Concepcion, Tarlac, eight soldiers assaulted the entourage of Mrs. Aquino's sister-in-law.

NAMFREL, the National Citizens Movement for Free Elections, had set up huge blackboards at Rizal Park to tally the count. By February 9, it was reporting a one-million-vote lead for Mrs. Aquino. Mrs. Aquino demanded that Marcos concede defeat and step down to preserve the peace. Not yet, said the government's Commission on Elections (COMELEC), which was reporting official returns at a snail's pace, prompting the U.S. observer team to comment that this was a deliberate attempt "to massage" the results. COMELEC, in turn, demanded to know where NAMFREL was getting its numbers.

"You would not believe how many people Radio Veritas fielded for the election," Jaime Cardinal Sin said. Although the church could not really "interfere in partisan politics," it did organize NAMFREL, giving the leadership to Jose Concepcion, head of the Council of the Laity. "We did this to ensure fair, honest, and clean elections," said the cardinal. "Politics is a human activity. And as a human activity, it has its morality." For his stand, the cardinal was berated as a Communist by Marcos's men; the church, as a feudal exploitative institution. "Marcos didn't like it because he was already thinking of doing some cheating, some deceiving."

Although Sin was not considered a theologian or philosopher on the level of the Jesuits, as archbishop of Manila and prince of the Catholic Church he wielded tremendous influence. "All during 1985, which was a Marian year, I traveled through the country exhorting people to penance. Our battle cry then was COR, which also means heart: C for conversion; O for offering one's self to God; and R for reparation. I took my inspiration from the Corinthians, where it is written that if God wanted to punish a people, he sent bad leaders. On the other hand, if the people turned to God and made reparations, then everything would be all right." To this end, the cardinal had urged Aquino and Laurel to come to an agreement. "It was so difficult for Doy [Laurel]," he said. "He'd been preparing for the presidency for two years. That morning of the COMELEC deadline for the filing of candidacy certificates, Cory [Aquino] came here and said she didn't want any political parties, she would run alone. I said to her, 'Child, you will lose; you have no experience, and you have no organization; your opponent is a very powerful man.' That same afternoon, Doy came with Jose Concepcion and Ernesto Maceda. He said to me, 'Why don't we have a box here and draw lots; whoever gets number one runs for president.' I said, 'Doy, this is not gambling!' Then I asked him, 'Do you love your country?' " Put that way, with the archbishop's miter and the cardinal's red hat before him, Laurel was struck as dumb as Job. "I told him, 'If you do, make this sacrifice, because Cory is more popular than you. If you do, look for her right now, come to an agreement, and go to COMELEC!' They made it forty minutes before the midnight deadline." The cardinal chuckled.

Tolentino was cynical about the arrangement. "I don't know the details," he said. "But Laurel was supposed to get a certain percentage of the cabinet appointments." The deal, however, freed the church to concentrate on the mechanics of the election. "I issued a pastoral letter," Cardinal Sin said, "telling people to accept money when it was offered but to go ahead and vote according to their conscience. To reject money when your children are starving—that's heroism. And heroism is not obligatory." Beyond that, the church placed its formidable resources at the service of NAMFREL and the opposition: two thousand schools with fifteen thousand teachers and more than a million students; sixteen radio stations; and a network of two thousand parishes with innumerable barrio chapels and social action centers. Most of the NAMFREL volunteers were squeaky-clean Catholic-school students and faculty members. "Our hundred and ten bishops got together and decided to back NAMFREL," the cardinal said. "Of course some were worried. 'What would happen if Marcos won?' they asked. 'He will come down hard on us.' But I told them, 'We're bishops!' " The cardinal's popularity is not general, however. A nun told me quietly that among some religious people, Cardinal Sin is regarded as "not a bishop but a politician." The cardinal's oft-stated motive for his actions—of "fighting communism"—did not sit well with the younger and more idealistic members of the church, who believed that the fight for justice needed no justification other than itself.

The period after the election may be divided into three phases: from February 7 to February 12, when Marcos appeared to be in control; then from February 13 to 15, when a stalemate ensued; then from February 15 on, when Aquino went on the offensive. As in any situation of great flux, there were overlaps in these phases—but what was notable was that, despite the high level of stridency on both sides, action rather than words remained the decisive factor in pushing developments toward one side or the other. As long as both limited themselves to blasting one another in the media— which incidentally turned the snap election into probably the most reported-on (in both print and broadcast) political exercise in the world—the state of affairs in the country remained equivocal, fluid, and unresolved.

In the first postelection phase, Marcos led in theatrics; he even challenged foreign correspondents to push-up contests when he was asked about his health. He met U.S. criticism of the election head on, hinting that he would void the election results. At the same time, he issued a subtle threat to the U.S. government: If Washington deemed his victory fraudulent, then the Americans should leave Clark Air Force Base and Subic Naval Base; the Philippine government would work out a modus vivendi with the Soviet Union. The threat resulted in Washington's equivocation. After twenty years of dealing with the United States, Marcos knew well what buttons to press to get the "proper" reaction. President Ronald Reagan qualified his judgment of the Philippine elections by saying that both sides cheated. A White House statement indicated that it expected Marcos to win the election.

Cardinal Sin jumped into the fray by issuing yet another letter, this one denouncing election frauds. Bayan, with its two million members, threatened massive protest actions. However, since COMELEC was the official referee of the contest and its count was proceeding inexorably, the protests were merely noises in the wind. COMELEC slapped a cease-and-desist order on NAMFREL.

On February 9, though, COMELEC itself was stopped when twenty-nine of its computer operators walked out, charging that there were discrepancies between their own counts and that of the central computer board. Nearly hysterical from their own daring and weeping from tension, the operators were mobbed by media people, U.S. embassy officials, and NAMFREL members. COMELEC had to stop its own count; its integrity was seriously compromised. By chance I met former National Press Club President Amando Doronila, who'd spent the last ten years in exile in Australia. "He's going to fall," he said, referring to Marcos. We went back and forth on how that could possibly be done, what process would make it happen. "That's the question," he finally said, "but he will fall nevertheless. It's only a matter of time."

Despite the confusion, life went on in all its mundane details. Weddings and baptisms, rites of passage in a Catholic agrarian country, were still being held. The only difference was that everyone everywhere talked politics, politics, politics. A top Marcos man celebrated his birthday, but even in the oasis of order that was his luxurious mansion, politics intruded. Red-and-white-clothed tables had been set up near an azure swimming pool, and a uniformed waiter served filet mignon and prawns. Since I was there as a "neutral" observer, I had no compunction about piling food on my plate; after a diet of coconut sap and strange leaves in peasant country, it was irresistible. The favored drink here was Royal Salute, at sixty dollars a bottle, duty free. Nothing disturbed the civilized flow of conversation except for the rustle of leaves in the trees and the stirring of water in the pool.

The talk naturally was about the election. "Wasn't that some vaudeville NAMFREL staged?" someone asked, referring to the COMELEC operators' walkout. "That had not been anticipated—the human factor," another explained.

Our host's aide, who could not be bothered to pay his employees early enough on February 5 so they could join Marcos's rally, gleefully mimicked Mrs. Aquino's pained reaction to the election frauds. "What did she expect?" he asked. "Only a stupid person would not ensure victory at the polls if he had the means. She actually expected Marcos not to cheat!" No one contradicted him; this was *realpolitik*. One kept one's power by any means.

But the confidence was merely a facade. Later, one of them approached me and, seeing to it that we would not be overheard, asked about his chances of acquiring permanent residency in the United States. My surprise must have been evident. "You won't have this over there," I said, gesturing at our surroundings. His face suddenly twisted, and he leaned back in his chair, stretching his body as if to rid himself of pain. "If it were just me," he said, "I wouldn't mind. I'd stay. But my wife, my kids—" Terror descended on his face, and I understood. He had sacrificed himself on Marcos's altar; what if it were demanded of him to sacrifice his family? The order and luxury that surrounded us were paid for—and would continue to be paid for—by self-loathing.

With COMELEC unable to continue its tally, the only alternative was to turn the process of determining who won over to the next higher body—the National Assembly, which responded by constituting itself into a national board of canvassers. A collective groan met the announcement. The Assembly was controlled by pro-Marcos men, from Speaker Nicanor Yñiguez on down; the opposition assemblymembers could only plan on a walkout when Marcos was proclaimed. *"Tapos na ang boksing* ('The boxing bout is over')," said an Aquino campaigner. Legions of Metro-Manila "aides"—street sweepers—were out in full force, scrubbing and scratching at campaign posters, peeling them off walls, electric posts, and garbage cans. It was comical to watch them tackle ten-foot walls layered in paper. They had only a small metal scraping device, wash rags, pails, and the ubiquitous coconut-rib brooms for equipment. Neverthe-

less, within seventy-two hours, the city's main thorough-
fares had been cleared of mementos of the snap election. It
was indecent, said a woman member of the Doctors for
Cory movement, the haste of this attempt to make people
forget what had transpired. She was as demoralized as
everybody else, she said. She hunched her shoulders to
show the weight of the defeat that Marcos was handing the
nation. None of them had expected the teachers who'd
manned the voting precincts to be bought off. "For two
thousand pesos," she said, mourning, "only two thousand
pesos!" But that was more than their monthly salary, I said
to her. "Is there no hope at all, no remedy?" she asked.

Gen. Fabian Ver, once again chief of staff of the armed
forces, lifted his red-alert order. Everything presumably
was going back to normal. The anticipation of victory gave
courage, it seemed, to a group of armed men, allegedly led
by a Philippine Constabulary captain, John Palay, and a former soldier called Boy Muslim. They murdered in broad
daylight Evelio Javier, former governor of Antique province.
His bullet-studded body was left in an outhouse, to which
the masked men had chased him. "Jesus Christ," said a university professor, "you get a Harvard education and die in a
toilet stall." But his death stoked the simmering rage again,
and while military tanks were being deployed quietly
around Malacanang Palace and in strategic spots in Metro-
Manila—no indication, said Ver, of any plan to reimpose
martial law—leaders of church, opposition, and cause-
oriented groups met to consider their next move.

Although 96 of 124 canvass certificates submitted to the
Assembly were found to have been tampered with, no one
was foolish enough to hope that the Assembly would not
proclaim Marcos the winner. Even if it did not, proving that
Mrs. Aquino won would have been a long and tedious
process. At best, the Assembly could have declared itself
unable to decide and nullified the election results—which
would have left Marcos still in charge. Very few were willing to accept that. Marcos must have realized the predica-
ment, for he offered to set up a Council of State that would

advise him on basic government policies. He asked Mrs. Aquino to join the council, at the same time saying he hoped she would abide by the rules and processes of the National Assembly.

Aquino's response was to reject any "power-sharing scheme" and to warn the U.S. president against conspiring with Marcos over the election. Calls for nationwide civil disobedience began to echo over the land, coinciding with declarations from both Defense Minister Juan Ponce Enrile and General Fidel Ramos that tensions were extremely high throughout the country, that the postelection period was a critical one. As if to punctuate the uncertainty, a team of International Monetary Fund negotiators, scheduled to arrive in Manila to discuss the country's maturing loans, postponed its visit.

When Reagan's envoy, Philip Habib, arrived in Manila, Aquino reportedly greeted him with a cool "and what can we do for you, Mr. Habib?" Reagan's statement that both sides cheated had hardened suspicion that the U.S. government was determined to keep Marcos in power. At every White House statement favoring Marcos, the opposition screamed, "Foreign intervention!" But other forces, deep within the bowels of the country, were already at work. Cardinal Sin had denounced election fraud, and the Catholic Bishops Conference of the Philippines (CBCP) was locked in a discussion of what position to take. The cause-oriented groups were firming up plans to paralyze the country. Aquino and Laurel called for another rally at Rizal Park, a show of force that would convince any observer that the nation had indeed gone oppositionist.

On February 15, Manila coffee shops buzzed with gossip about a predawn visit by Imelda Romualdez-Marcos to the residence of the archbishop of Manila. The irrepressible cardinal was reported to have asked the "Ma'am" what she was doing at that unholy hour in "the house of Sin." Mrs. Marcos asked the cardinal to use his influence to stop the CBCP from condemning the conduct of the election. Cardinal Sin said he had only one vote within the CBCP, that it was Ricardo Cardinal Vidal who was its head, and that it was too late anyway; a three-man committee had already drafted the statement. The "Ma'am" threw herself to the floor and had a fit. Then she rushed off to see Cardinal Vidal, who said the same thing: It was too late. Again, the "Ma'am" threw herself to the floor, wringing her hands. "She was auditioning for the lead in *La Traviata*," said the high school teacher who recounted the incident to me.

The wind of desperation was blowing toward the Marcos camp now. Ronald Reagan turned around and said it was the ruling party that had perpetuated the fraud. *"Patay na siya* ('He's dead')," the teacher added, gleefully clasping his hands above his head. The U.S. Cavalry was riding to the rescue. Later, a U.S. embassy official waxed indignant when I asked about this confusion in policy. "Who was confused?" he demanded. "We weren't. We knew what we were doing from the very beginning. Only one man woke up too early in the morning and didn't know what was going on." He grinned.

On February 16, more than a million people gathered once more at Rizal Park. It was here that Auxiliary Bishop of Manila Teodoro Bacani read the CBCP statement: " 'According to moral principles, a government that assumes or retains power through fraudulent means has no moral basis. . . . If such a government does not of itself freely correct the evil it has inflicted on the people, then it is our serious moral obligation to make it do so.' " A month later to the day, around twenty bishops met at the Ateneo University's Pollock Retreat Center and mulled over those words. Despite the statement's emphasis on nonviolent means in confronting the state, the bishops, the gathering agreed, "did call for a revolution"—an act that threw the church into the center stage of partisan politics. The possibility of the overt use of church power and influence to change the country's development had equally tantalized and repelled many a church worker for years. It was tantalizing, since it could resolve so many problems; it was repelling, because the church had started in the country as an oppressive adjunct of colonial power. The gathered bishops concluded that the CBCP statement was a dangerous precedent.

But in the crowd now, this February 16, the atmosphere was once again festive. Yellow banners competed with the golden yellow of the sun. Swelled by legions from cause-oriented groups, the rally was bigger than the Aquino-Laurel *miting de avance*. More than that, it was a reunion of friends; itinerant vendors were out in full force; entertainers were present; and soutaned priests dreamily eyed what could be the largest congregation for a parish. I was strolling through the crowd copying hand-lettered signs that mostly denounced Marcos as a thief and a dictator when my companion, a former political prisoner, gave a cry: "What is Major Castillo doing up there?" he demanded. The man, speared by our glance, froze on the backstage ladder, slipped through the crowd, and came toward us. He slung his walkie-talkie discreetly at his waistband, threw his arms around my friend, muttered, *"Kumusta* ('How are you')?" and then disappeared into a knot of people. My friend scanned the crowd around the stage, indicated half a dozen men squatting at strategic spots, and pulled me away. "Let's get out of here," he said. "Those are the Camp Crame killers." "Camp Crame killers" was a label used by those who had undergone "tactical interrogation" at the charnel houses of the military camp. "Stay away from the stage," he advised, "it might explode!" No one had forgotten the August 21, 1971, blowing up of the Liberal Party's *miting de avance* at Plaza Miranda. Mystified by the presence of soldiers in plainclothes, we walked through the crowd. Aquino was onstage asking the nation to boycott the products of Marcos crony–owned corporations. It seemed easy to do until the crowd realized that *crony–owned* included the San Miguel Corporation, and if there was anything Filipinos loved, it was San Miguel beer. A collective groan went up; a nearby bunch of teenagers fervently discussed what brand could replace San Miguel. "Oh, no! We'll have to drink Manila beer!" one cried out in mock sorrow. Aquino had no idea what kind of sacrifice she was demanding.

Boycotting products meant nothing to Toti and Alicia, who were once again doing a brisk trade. Toti wished he had yellow T-shirts to sell, while Alicia, having sold her garlands, was bored to death. But they hung on, ogling celebrities and looking for popular singer Kuh Ledesma. Both said they did not expect Marcos to leave the Palace. But if he did, Toti promised to smoke his daily allotment of three cigarettes one after another. "I will celebrate," he said, raising his voice in the next instant to cry out, "*Yosi, yosi* ('Cigarettes')." If the election disturbances went on, he joked, he might yet become a millionaire by selling cigarettes to the crowds. But really all he wanted was a Sony Walkman and a pair of long pants. He was getting to be too big for his cutoffs. Alicia evaded dreams; she wanted nothing, she said. "You are too young not to have dreams," I told her. She looked away and muttered that perhaps she could stop selling flowers and go to school.

"We had no doubt at all that we could force Marcos to step down," Laurel would say later. "But doing it through the civil disobedience movement would have taken a long time. *Matagal* ('Too long'). We were prepared, however, to go on to the bitter end." Despite his statement then that Marcos would fall in three weeks, other opposition leaders were estimating that it would take at least three months of consistent and total noncooperation with the government to force the issue. They took comfort, however, from noises emanating from Washington, where U.S. congressmen and senators were demanding that Marcos step down. The embattled President Marcos threatened once more to abrogate the bases treaty between the Philippines and the United States if the latter cut off aid to his regime. He also announced General Ver's resignation and the appointment of General Ramos as chief of staff. But in the next instant he rescinded his own decision, saying that Ver would be staying until March 1—by which time, presumably, Marcos's hold on another term of office would be secure. Ramos complained that the confusion about who was actually in command was making the armed forces unstable.

Hardly anyone noticed the National Assembly's proclamation of Marcos as president-elect and of Tolentino as vice president-elect. It intruded into the national attention only when Marcos set his inauguration for February 25 at Rizal Park. "It was going to be the bash to end all bashes," a Malacanang Palace insider said. News of the inaugural rites set coffee shop habitues wondering how many gowns Mrs. Marcos would order from which couturier (the final tally was five, from Ballestra and Pitoy Moreno—excluding those for her daughters Imee and Irene) and who would be the "guests" at the inauguration. Manila's diplomatic community had ignored the presidential victory; a dead silence had met the Assembly's proclamation. Only the Soviet ambassador was tricked into felicitations. He had been presenting his credentials to Marcos when the latter mentioned his re-election. The reluctant diplomat had no choice but to congratulate the man—which the Marcos press seized upon and trumpeted. That did not make up for the general snubbing of Marcos by the international community, whose ambassadors and consuls trickled steadily to Aquino's house and campaign headquarters. Some had been recalled by their governments, and others asked to be called "for consultations" in their home countries to avoid the presidential inauguration. This, said the incessantly gossiping coffee shop crowd, left only the "Ma'am's" jet-setting circle as guests. "Expect Christina Ford then," said a beer-guzzling wag at a Makati lounge. "Maybe a comtessa or two. Christiaan Barnard—yes? And, oh! Don't forget George Hamilton, dahling Georgie-orgie." Everybody guffawed.

But was there no way to stop the inauguration? At this, eyes shied away, glasses and cups were lifted, and a palpable darkness descended. "We Filipinos will never make it," a young businessman said grimly. At another coffee shop, a friend who'd worked intermittently for both the Marcos and the Aquino camp (yes, a few managed to straddle both worlds) got hysterical when he saw me. "What are you doing here?" he said. "You're crazy. Get out, get out tomorrow—today, if possible." What was he talking about? "It will be the worst-case scenario," he blubbered. "The generals will move." But which ones, and how? "Who knows?" he said, airily. "All of them. Every single one of them." But by that Friday, it was common knowledge that Minister of Defense Juan Ponce Enrile was resigning "irrevocably."

"I called all the experts," Cardinal Sin said. "The Dominicans, the Jesuits, and some lay people. I'd been telling everybody that Cory would win. Nobody believed me. So we sat down and considered what could happen. One scenario after another was presented. If Cory wins, will Marcos allow her to take over? What if, what if, what if. . . . Finally we decided that five scenarios were the most probable, and we worked out our possible response to each. And then when something did happen, it was none of the five. It was marked NONE OF THE ABOVE. And I had no ready response, after all that effort. There was no time to gather people to advise me. I was alone here [at the archbishop's residence]. I had to decide on my own."

SEVEN

*To Coup or
Not to Coup*

Time has edited the accounts of those who were at the center of the last three days of the three-year revolt against Marcos (if one locates its beginning as the Aquino assassination, though the process began long before that). The details of what happened at the instant of its happening may never be revealed, because in the post-Marcos period, the scramble for power and position has imposed its own logic on memories. Heroics have been blown up, while seamier actions have been veiled.

Two things have to be kept in mind when those three days that saw the end of the Marcos regime are recalled. First, political decisions and destinies in the Philippines are worked out by a small circle of men and women in negotiations to which the general public is not privy. And second, many of those at the political storm center of those days had matured in the Marcos era; they bore his stamp.

However, what has not been edited or altered by the intervening months is that nameless men and women, heedless of their own powerlessness and anonymity, insisted by their sheer presence alone that they be part of the equation of change this time in what was, after all, the only country they would ever have. That part of the "revolution" remains pristine, despite the clouds that have since descended.

Friday, February 21, dawned no differently from previous days for Danilo Galang, thirty-five years old, a Catholic school teacher—except for a flurry of indecision occasioned by information from his brother, a class of 1973 Philippine Military Academy graduate. Earlier, his brother had received a call advising him to remove his family from the city because the Reform the Armed Forces of the Philippines Movement (RAM) was planning to do "something" that weekend. This tip-off was passed on to relatives, and Galang took "precautionary measures," calling up a few friends to warn them. He assumed—or rather hoped—that whatever RAM was planning would take place between Saturday evening and Sunday. "As it turned out," he said, "the RAM operational plan called for an early Saturday morning execution."

According to Arturo Tolentino, information that surfaced after the revolt showed that RAM had planned a coup for midnight, February 21, after the departure of Philip Habib. For some reason, the latter was delayed—which caused the coup's postponement to Saturday, February 22. "When history is written," said Tolentino, "it will show that no revolution took place here, that what we had was a military mutiny abetted by civilian protection." The earliest account of the revolt traced its beginning to the arrest of the security detail of Commerce and Trade Minister Roberto Ongpin. On their way back from escorting the minister to his suburban home, the security detail was abruptly surrounded and encircled by Scout rangers. They were then taken to Fort Bonifacio, headquarters of the Philippine Army, whose commanding officer was an associate of General Ver. Several explanations were subsequently offered for the arrest; Enrile himself said that the men had been conducting evening exercises with firearms. Since the site for the "exercises" turned out to be a restricted zone under Philippine Marines control, it was a curious thing. Col. Mariano Santiago said flat out that there had been a coup attempt; the men were probing the Marines' defense perimeter.

When it became apparent that no one really cared how Marcos had been gotten rid of, as long as he was out, elaborations on the tale from various military men further amended the story. A coup had been "in the works" since 1985, and the defense minister only joined it in 1986. And Enrile himself claimed that behind the Reform the Armed Forces Movement was yet another organization preparing for a coup. His resignation was supposed to become valid on February 24, and simultaneous provincial mutinies by military forces were supposed to take place on the twenty-eighth, as a prelude to a general revolt.

However, whether he knew it or not, an attack on the Palace had been planned by his hot-headed young subalterns. From three launching points, commando teams were to cross the Pasig River and "capture" the president. The Palace itself had been primed with land mines. The intention, a young officer said later, had not been to kill the president but to make him resign.

Who or what was on top of this plan, no one has yet revealed. Very few knew about it; certainly the U.S. embassy, which had been in touch with RAM since its formation in 1985, did, though it had doubts about the plan's efficiency. What all the stories added up to was that "something" had indeed been planned—a long time before anyone smelled it. That explained the presence of the Camp Crame soldiers at Aquino's last rally in Manila.

Later, Col. Gregorio Honasan, Enrile's senior military aide, confirmed that contacts had been initiated with the Aquino camp even before election day, February 7. A nervous military man said only that "there were a lot of mouselike scuttlings in the dark." Coincidentally, Aquino and Laurel had left Manila for Cebu City, in a central Philippine island, that weekend. Laurel said that neither he nor Mrs. Aquino had had an inkling of what was about to happen.

One of Minister Ongpin's bodyguards managed to get to a telephone and called him. The minister thereupon called Marcos, who assured him he would have the matter investigated. Meanwhile, the president said, Ongpin could have a new set of bodyguards from the presidential security unit. Ongpin, made nervous by the thought of having Ver's men about him, refused. He recorded an account of the incident and went to bed. The next morning he called Enrile, who had given him his security detail.

Enrile was at his usual morning haunt, the Atrium Coffee Shop, when he was told that Ongpin was on the phone. Apprised of the previous evening's events, Enrile called his office. After receiving a plausible explanation for the arrest, he returned to his table. He stayed awhile, waiting to see if anything would turn up. Then he went to his house at a nearby exclusive subdivision for lunch. Colonels Honasan and Eduardo Kapunan, both RAM steering committee members, arrived shortly thereafter and informed the minister that Ver had organized arrest teams to round up the estimated four hundred officers in Metro-Manila who were RAM members.

It was a do-or-die moment. The three decided that their best chance was to regroup and hole up at Camp Aguinaldo, where the defense ministry was located. Enrile called Gen. Fidel Ramos and told him of the danger. Was the general with them? "All the way, sir!" In which case, Enrile said, the general should meet them at Camp Aguinaldo. Enrile and his two colonels then took a helicopter—though not before the defense minister had packed a bag and slung on his favorite weapon, an Israeli Ghalil Uzi, with which most of his men were armed.

From his office, Enrile called U.S. Ambassador Stephen Bosworth and Japanese Ambassador Kikoshi Somiya and informed them of the situation. It was a move that would stalemate Marcos and eventually carry the day for the mutineers. The U.S. ambassador threatened to cut off aid totally to the Marcos regime, win or lose, should the president use American-supplied heavy military hardware to crush the revolt. "It wasn't as civilized as all that," a Palace insider said, chuckling. "Bosworth and Marcos were shrieking at each other. And they would shriek at each other some more." Enrile also called his wife and told her to get in touch with Cardinal Sin and *Inquirer* publisher Eugenia Apostol.

The same Palace person said that Enrile's alleged investment in the newspaper had been a sore point with the Marcos people and had exacerbated Marcos's distrust of his minister. "The problem with the 'Sir,' " he added, "was he was too soft. He was very reluctant to fire anyone close to him. Even in the case of the cronies, he knew they had made money many times over what he owed them. But he simply did not have the heart to stop them; nor even to stop Enrile. Perhaps because of his illness or, then again, perhaps they were the last to treat him with a show of respect and affection. Or most probable, he was trying to keep them for the 'Ma'am's' protection after—well—after his demise."

Jaime Cardinal Sin was not at his San Miguel archbishop's palace when Mrs. Enrile called at about four in the afternoon. But she left word of what was happening. Meanwhile, back at Camp Aguinaldo, Enrile had scheduled a press conference for 6:00 P.M. and was waiting impatiently for Ramos. The cardinal reached his home at about six and was informed of Mrs. Enrile's call. Since a group of RAM officers had paid the cardinal a visit the week before, he knew "something of them." Still, he could not make up his mind. He was mulling things over when the defense minister called, followed by General Ramos. The cardinal asked both to wait. He needed time to think, to come to a decision.

The portly cardinal, usually of high spirits and great optimism, was thrown into a tizzy by all the telephone calls. Before anything else, he himself did some telephoning—not to his political experts, but to the Contemplative sisters, the *monjas* who hardly ever left their cells and spent their lives in silence, in convent work, in meditation, and in prayer. The cardinal asked the sisters of the three Contemplative orders in Manila to leave their rooms and go to their respective chapels. They should prostrate themselves before the altar and pray. As soon as all the sisters were in position, the cardinal should be informed.

Around two hundred RAM members secured Camp Aguinaldo, whose military police commander, Brig. Gen. Pedro Balbanero, had been convinced to stay neutral in the coming confrontation. Media men started pouring into the camp, hefting cameras and lights. The conference itself started late because Ramos had been delayed. Before an oversize crowd of local and foreign media men, Enrile and Ramos announced their revolt and said that they believed Marcos had not won the February 7 election.

Luis Teodoro had just returned home from editing stories—"the usual ones about human rights violations, summary executions, and arrests by the military"—and filing them with an ecumenical news agency he worked with secretly, when a university faculty member came knocking to tell him that Enrile and Ramos had barricaded themselves at Camp Aguinaldo. "I turned on the radio, tuned in to Radio Veritas, and there they were. Enrile was saying that his and Ramos's arrests had been ordered because of a supposed coup plot against Marcos. He implied that this was just an excuse and the plot was nonexistent. He kept saying 'we will die here' whenever he was asked how long he and Ramos planned to hold out. He seemed hysterical and scared, whereas Ramos was more sure of himself and was appealing to field commanders and officers to withdraw their support from Marcos.

"Enrile was on the air for about ten minutes, saying that Marcos had cheated in the election, that he himself had helped Marcos cheat by 350,000 votes in his home region Cagayan, and that the ambush of his car in 1972, which was used to justify the declaration of martial law, had been stage-managed." Despite the general surprise, few could not help smiling at Enrile's naïveté. Everyone knew his car's ambush had been faked. Late television news reports on that September 20 had flashed a photo of a totaled car with no mention of fatalities, implying that crazed guerrillas had assaulted a parked and empty car.

Monico Atienza, who'd been beaten to a pulp during his arrest and detention by the military, was resting at a friend's apartment when the phone rang. It was six-thirty in the afternoon, he remembered, when the caller advised him to turn on the radio to hear something interesting. "I did and heard Enrile saying this was a last stand against the dictatorship, that Marcos had cheated in the election. Then Ramos made an appeal to the people, especially to Cardinal Sin and other church elements, to please send food, medicine, and other things, and if possible to ring Camp Aguinaldo with people. He used the term *people power* at this point."

The cardinal could hardly keep still in his residence. He went to the chapel to pray, tormented by visions of bloodshed all over Manila. Forty minutes after giving the sisters his instructions, he called them again, order by order. "Are you all in the chapel?" he asked the sisters, who answered yes. "Are you in position?" he asked again to make sure. Yes. "Pray, then, that there will be no violence." Cardinal Sin then went on the air to ask the people to support Enrile and Ramos. Bring food, he said; the soldiers are hungry and have no food. Protect them, protect them. In less than twenty minutes, he said, they came running.

"My immediate reaction," said Teodoro, "was that he was treating the people like cannon fodder." Elsewhere, leaders of "the parliament of the streets" broke out in a cold sweat at the thought of unarmed and hapless civilians rammed to death by tanks, raked by gunfire, and clubbed bloody by Marcos's soldiers. Their experience with Marcos's troops in street demonstrations had not been at all pleasant. "I had no doubt Marcos would have the crowd brutalized," said a squatters' area organizer. "It was a peculiar dilemma. Should you ignore the appeals and let a massacre take place, or should you lead your people there, unarmed and defenseless, knowing they could be massacred themselves?" He decided to go to the camps and check the situation out for himself.

According to Leto Villar of Kilusang Mayo Uno (KMU), the labor group, KMU leaders were locked in conference at the Silahis Hotel with leaders of rival unions when news of the Enrile-Ramos mutiny came via a phone call. "The worker and peasant sectors," Villar said, "were gearing for a nationwide people's strike. As organized forces, these sectors, especially the workers, had the capability to launch a full-scale strike within twenty-four hours. Bayan leaders were already spreading out to various regions and provinces to coordinate with various groups there. We at the KMU, on the other hand, took the initiative to have this secret consultation. Secret, because this was still the Marcos era. So that night of the mutiny, the leaders of the largest unions were meeting to finalize plans for a general strike on the twenty-fifth, leading to a coordinated support of Mrs. Aquino's civil disobedience movement."

The KMU leaders did not think that a simple boycott of crony-owned corporations would be as effective as a general people's strike. But they had to go through the meetings carefully, because the other unions did not wish to come out in the open—"like the Federation of Free Workers and one wing of the Trade Union Council of the Philippines." The latter was the only recognized labor center under the Marcos regime.

The call—from a media friend—reached Villar in the middle of the meeting. "We were stunned," he said, "but the news speeded up the deliberations. Suddenly everybody agreed: Strike! It was rather funny. We agreed and then separated." Villar himself had just returned from Cebu. He hadn't realized he'd taken the same plane from Manila as Laurel. "So when I reached Cebu, there was a band there," he said, laughing, "and a welcoming crowd. I thought it was for me, but then Doy [Laurel] appeared. *Ay, mali* ['a mistake']!" After checking on preparations for the strike in Cebu, he went back to Manila for the meeting.

"Despite news of the mutiny, I still flew to Bicol province," he said, "to coordinate with the transport workers there for the strike."

In Cebu City, Cory Aquino was announcing the formation of several committees that would eventually become part of her cabinet—to make sure that "when Ferdinand Marcos goes, we will be ready to take over." She was with her brother, Jose Cojuangco; former Constitutional Convention delegate and Cagayan de Oro Mayor Aquilino Pimentel; and former Congressman Ramon Mitra, when news of the mutiny came. They decided to call Manila and were alarmed when they could not get through to Camp Aguinaldo. They had to try over and over again until they finally got a connection to Enrile's office. What could she do for the minister and the general? Aquino asked. "Just pray for us" was the answer. U.S. Consul Blaine Porter arrived at that point and promised to check with the Manila embassy on what Aquino's options were.

Col. Mariano Santiago's immediate reaction on hearing of the mutiny was that "this was it"—the long-rumored plan to make Enrile the head of government. At the same time, he thought it could be turned into "the push" that would "hasten Corazon C. Aquino's ascension as seventh president of the Republic of the Philippines." Ever since his attempt to break up a car-napping ring that had been protected by a general, Santiago had been on the outs with the regime and had worked for the Aquino campaign. He immediately dialed Radio Veritas's phone number because he wanted to call on the people to go to Camp Aguinaldo and create a buffer zone between the Enrile-Ramos and Marcos troops. Unfortunately, Radio Veritas's phones were humming, and he could not get through. Instead, he got several phone calls himself from friends in the Cory Aquino for President Movement, asking what they should do. He told them to call up other friends and to keep listening to Radio Veritas. He would relay instructions through the Catholic Church radio.

"I decided to go to the station," said Santiago, "and

found Father Larry, retired Colonel Philip Carreon, and Harry Gasser there." There were unconfirmed reports that the offices of the newspapers *Malaya* and *Inquirer* had been raided. "I tried to convince Father Larry that the time to call for people's support had come. But he was hesitant because he did not want to alarm the people unduly."

Monico Atienza was still glued to the radio at eight in the evening and heard Agapito "Butz" Aquino call for people to assemble at the Cubao shopping center, near both Camps Crame and Aguinaldo. Agapito said everyone would march at the same time along Epifanio de los Santos Avenue (EDSA) toward the two camps. "I was still thoroughly confused by what was going on," Atienza said. "Was this real, or a trick by the dictator? I called a half dozen of my students. They were quite excited by what was happening and were listening to the radio. I told them that perhaps we should heed the appeals made by Cardinal Sin, Butz, Ramos, and Enrile. They told me that they and their families were on their way to Cubao. I then called several nephews and nieces, relatives and provincemates. They were also about to leave for Cubao, but they warned me to stay away. Whatever happened, they would tell me. I told them all right, but I decided to sneak to Cubao myself. There I saw a thick crowd gathered in front of Isetann [a department store]—the middle class, the community youths, the curious, and some familiar faces from cause-oriented groups who, however, were not carrying their organizations' banners. Of course, the 'star' was Butz and his ATOM group. I did not proceed to Aguinaldo and instead went home. A friend arrived, and we spent up to four in the morning discussing what was going on. Was this a coup? Was the Central Intelligence Agency involved? Will the cause-oriented groups join in?"

Fr. Jose Dizon, who—along with members of Bayan Southern Luzon—had served as Mrs. Aquino's pollwatcher during the election, said that although the organization was unable to respond to the February 22 events systematically, individual members did react to the aired appeals. He was there himself at EDSA that evening. "Understand that Bayan could not adjust to the sudden turnaround of Enrile and Ramos," he said. Still, almost against their better judgment, Bayan members went to the camps—if only to see what was going on.

Toti and Alicia were home in their squatter's shack when the radio began blaring the voices of Enrile and Ramos, followed by Cardinal Sin and an assortment of celebrities. They looked at each other. Toti's first impulse was to pick up his cigarette box. Wherever people gathered, cigarettes could be sold. But the next instant, he put it down again, his eyes bulging from the thought that this was the military. *"Militar ito* ('this is the military')," he remembered saying to himself. Like most street vendors, his contact with uniformed men—"police, soldiers, security guards—*parepareho 'yan basta may baril* ('they're all alike, as long as they have guns')"—had been unpleasant, limited to extortionate demands for loose change or cigarettes, accompanied by a cuff on the head or two. Alicia, silent, watched her older brother. The whole house was silent except for the blaring of the radio. For the first time, no one knew what to do.

The American photojournalist Charlyn Zlotnick noticed frenetic activity at the Associated Press and found out what was going on. She grabbed her cameras and hailed a taxicab, but the driver refused to go beyond Cubao. She started walking, lugging her camera bag and silently cursing the cab driver, her cameras, and her fate as a photographer. "I'd reached the corner where the Aguinaldo walls started," she recalled, "and I was nearly dead from my equipment's weight. Then a military car came; I assumed it was checking defenses around the camp's perimeter. I leaned towards the driver's window and asked the young officer—who was in civvies—if he could give me a lift. He said sure, and I climbed in. He asked me for a cigarette. I never found out his name, but later I would see him in snappy uniform standing beside the defense minister. Once he smiled at me and asked if I remembered him. I surely did. He took me to the front gate, which was already guarded. I could not get in. I thought I would position myself atop the wall, thinking that if anything came down the road I would have a panoramic view. I did not realize it was impossible to balance on the wall, that once up there, there was no recourse except to jump to the other side. So there I was, inside the camp. I made for the defense ministry building."

Col. Honesto Isleta, who had retired from the military after several years as a "floating officer"—that is, he had no command because he would not give in to pressure from above—was peaceably fulfilling his duties as a father that evening. "I had no inkling at all that something was happening," he said. "I knew that the minister of defense had been losing his powers and authority, that General Ver was going direct to Marcos. But I did not want to get involved in politics anymore. I had been bitter toward the military until last year, when I became a born-again Christian and let go of the emotion. But when Mrs. Aquino started calling for a civil disobedience movement, I did ask myself: If she does this, what will stop people from doing it for their own ends?"

So that night, Isleta had attended a concert where his daughter was performing and had gone to Broadway Centrum to have dinner. When he returned home with his wife, it was about eight o'clock. There was a knock at the door; his neighbor had sent over a maid to tell him to tune in to Radio Veritas. The first voice he heard was Enrile's; the second, Ramos's. "If it had been only Enrile, then that would have been nothing more than a political dissension. But General Ramos—he was seceding from the commander in chief!"

He and his wife alternated between the radio and the television. After hearing Cardinal Sin and Agapito "Butz" Aquino, Isleta suggested they go to Radio Veritas. His wife countered with a suggestion that they go to Camp Aguinaldo. Knowing the dangers attendant to a mutiny, Isleta refused. His wife pouted, sulked, turned her back, and refused to talk to him. *"Masama na ito* ('This is getting heavy'),'' he said to himself. *"Ayaw nang kumibo* ('She doesn't want to talk anymore').'' Finally he said okay, they were going to the camp. They passed the house of a couple who were their close friends. "The lights were off," Isleta said, "and there was no car in the driveway. But for some reason, I had the impulse to ask them to come along." So he rang the doorbell. The couple weren't asleep yet, and readily agreed to join the expedition.

Isleta parked his car on Eighteenth Avenue, some distance from Camp Aguinaldo. But when they reached the gate, they were told by the soldier stationed there that the camp had been sealed off. They were about to leave when an officer arrived, recognized Isleta, and asked if he wanted to see the minister. He nodded and told his wife to stay put with his friends. "It was fortuitous," he said. "If the other couple had not been with us, I would not have left my wife, I would not have gone in." He found Enrile preparing for his second press conference. "Congratulations," Isleta told the minister. He hung around for a while, chatting with the gathered officers, and then decided to cross the street to Camp Crame. He was about to congratulate Ramos when the general looked up, said, "Nes! Why don't you improve on this?" and handed him the statement he was preparing for the press conference. That was it; Isleta was back in the military.

At Fort Bonifacio, Jose Ma. Sison was listening to the radio in his maximum security cell when he heard the voices of Enrile and Ramos. In one of those leaps of political intuition that had made him a visionary, Sison turned to the cell window and shouted in the direction of other incommunicado prisoners, "Crisis! Confrontation! We will be released!"

One by one, a cluster of generals arrived at Enrile's office to offer their support: former Chief of Staff Romeo Espino; Brig. Gen. Ramon Farolan, who announced his resignation from the Customs Commission; Roilo Golez, who announced his resignation as postmaster general; and Brig.

Gen. Manuel Flores. Although Enrile felt that the situation was stable, the possibility of their total "annihilation could not be discounted."

At this point, Col. Rolando Abadilla, a Marcos emissary, arrived and asked Enrile to go with him to Malacanang Palace. The president wished to speak to him. Enrile refused, saying that all bridges had been burned and that they had already taken a stand. Colonel Abadilla was a known Marcos man, ruthless and skilled in his service to the president. An intelligence officer of the Metropolitan Command, he had been implicated in several torture cases, as well as in election frauds in Tagaytay, where an unknown protégé of Mrs. Marcos's partisan, Jose Conrado Benitez, had managed to win despite local antipathy. Now Abadilla left, only to return shortly, saying that Marcos still wanted to speak to Enrile. The latter refused, feeling that after twenty-one years he knew the president well enough not to fall into the trap. Abadilla then asked if Enrile would talk to General Ver. The minister said sure. So the Palace was rung up, and Enrile found himself in a classic exchange with the dour general.

"Sir," Ver reportedly said, "we were surprised by this turn of events."

"Well," Enrile countered, "I was informed you were trying to have us all arrested."

"That's not true," Ver replied, "that's not true. There were no such plans at all, no such orders."

"Well, anyway, the die is cast," Enrile said. "We have broken the shell of the egg, and the only thing left to do is to stir it." However, he cleverly interposed that it was too late to discuss things, so they had better wait for morning to talk about the problem. But if General Ver wished to talk in the morning, he should not give orders for an attack on the camps. His men "were ready to die to a man," and though their position was defensive, they would not hesitate to fight back if attacked.

There was a short pause and then Ver said, "May I also

ask you to commit to us that you will not attack the Palace tonight?"

Enrile gave his "solemn word" that his men would not, that they had "no aggressive intention against the Palace." He promised Ver that he and his men would confine themselves to the camp perimeter until morning, at which time the two would converse again.

Ver's request for a nonattack pledge, said a military man in postrevolt analysis, showed the Enrile-Ramos people his full measure. "Ver had never been in a combat situation," he said. "His responsibilities had been mostly defense and protection. So he could only move by surprise, pouncing on those who were against his boss. Or establishing a 'cleared' cordon of safety within which the Marcos family could move. With the first method no longer possible, he could only stick to the second. As soon as he asked for that commitment, we knew he was going to lay down a static defense position around the Palace. That would be his first move."

For Marcos's part, a Palace insider said, the president was taken aback by the minister's refusal to talk. It upset him thoroughly because in the last twenty years none of his people had ever refused him anything. He was not used to being reminded that he was merely a human being. The only solution he could come up with was to launch a propaganda war against the rebelling faction; he had little doubt he would win because—probably for the first time as president—he would be telling the truth.

The Palace called a press conference, and Marcos presented three officers who were allegedly part of the coup plot. "All three were with the presidential security," recalled Teodoro, "and even on television, they were visibly sweating." Capt. Ricardo Morales was made to read his confession. The coup plan called for commando raiders to cross the Pasig River and to assault the Palace. Three battalions and many officers, mostly RAM members, were involved. Although Marcos called both Enrile and Ramos "slay plotters," he said there was no evidence to link them to the coup. No warrants had been issued for their arrests. He said the two should "stop this foolishness" and end the hostility so that "we may negotiate." Otherwise, he would pulverize them with heavy artillery and tanks.

From what he'd heard, Isleta said, it seemed that two of Enrile's security people had been arrested and that there had been a leak of the Palace attack plan. The Palace had had its own postelection scenario drawn up. On Monday, General Ver's son Irwin was to be promoted to general; on Tuesday, Enrile, Ramos, and the RAM people were to be arrested, along with Mrs. Aquino's advisers and the leaders of opposition and cause-oriented groups. By Friday, martial law was to be reimposed all over the land. That Marcos credited Ver's son with the discovery of the coup plot is circumstantial evidence that the scenario was to be at least partially implemented. That Enrile's refusal to take his calls had humiliated Marcos was obvious. "Imagine," he said on television, "they won't even accept my phone calls!"

Enrile and Ramos worked out a perfect division of labor. While the defense minister faced the media and handled the political and propaganda aspects of the revolt, Ramos was on the phone covering the operational aspect, obtaining commitments of support from commanding and field officers. If someone could not be convinced to give active support, Ramos argued him into neutrality. Meanwhile, from Enrile's home province, Cagayan, one hundred officers and men who had served with the defense minister for some time were heading for Manila by truck and bus—or by helicopter, whenever possible. They had an arms stockpile, the result of the previous December's Operation Pegasus, a counterinsurgency exercise that incidentally secured Cagayan's shores for weapons shipment.

The initial response to the Enrile-Ramos appeals was not as massive as propaganda would have it. Their twenty years of service to Marcos did not exactly render them trustworthy. Only a few thousands made it to the camp, largely to deliver goods. But the Palace—hampered equally by the "honor among thieves" code and by the U.S. embassy's ultimatum—could not move. Enrile would later say that the first twelve hours in such a situation were the most decisive. With no buffer about the camps that Saturday evening and Sunday morning, Ver could have struck quickly and smashed the mutiny. But a Marcos man said that the president was also jittery about his security. That, said an opposition man, was the most probable explanation for the Ver troops' paralysis that Saturday morning.

"I remember [slain Antique Governor] Evelio Javier telling me," recalled a physicist, "that Marcos is a physical coward. When that bomb exploded near him at the ASTA convention in 1981, Javier said the president just fell down and froze. He could not move at all and had to be carried out bodily."

Still, Enrile admitted later, it was a low moment for him and his men; he kept getting a feeling of unreality, that everything that was happening was merely a bad dream. As the night deepened, the soldiers prepared to rest without taking off their shoes.

Charlyn Zlotnick, cameras still slung about her, found a large room in the defense ministry that had been designated the media room. Men and women were flung about on chairs and couches and piled on the floor, huddling together for warmth. She was about to lie down herself when a huge Caucasian entered, threw down his cameras, dove into the pile of bodies on the floor. "You should have seen this," she said. "Nobody moved. And there he was, completing the circle of bodies on the floor." It seemed an omen of things to come, this confusion of comatose bodies. As she prepared herself for sleep, her last thought was of Marcos saying he would pulverize the camp.

In Cebu City the Aquino group faced a different dilemma. U.S. Consul Blaine Porter had offered Mrs. Aquino accommodations aboard a U.S. destroyer that was docked by chance at the harbor. In the morning it could ferry her back to Manila. After a short discussion, they decided it would be unseemly for Mrs. Aquino, in whose name the mutiny was being waged, to arrive at the country's national capital aboard a U.S. warship. Aquino chose to spend the night at a Carmelite convent. "If the truth be told," said an Aquino campaigner, "at this point, no one trusted anybody."

EIGHT

*Onward to
the Barricades*

The group with Corazon C. Aquino had decided to burrow in Cebu City for one week, said Homobono Adaza, a former member of the National Assembly and an Aquino-Laurel campaigner. "They felt that what was happening was something orchestrated by Marcos, with the collusion of Enrile and Ramos, and the ultimate goal was to arrest the core of the opposition." Adaza, who had maintained his friendship with Enrile despite his oppositionist stand, had a different evaluation. "I insisted that, if not Mrs. Aquino and Mr. Laurel themselves, the opposition leaders about them should fly to Manila immediately. I told them if they did not do so, a new government would be formed, and the opposition won't be part of it." He himself was prepared to fly back and talk to the two rebelling leaders; he made arrangements with businessman Ernie Aboitiz to be piloted from Lahug Airport, then to Argao, and from there to Tagbilaran, where businessman Jaime Zobel's private plane would pick him up. But on the twenty-third, as he was about to execute the plan, he was told that the plane had been commandeered by other Aquino leaders. He had to take an afternoon Philippine Airlines jet.

"The morning of the twenty-fourth," he recounted, "we had a meeting at the Laurel compound. All of the opposition leaders were there, and so were Mrs. Aquino and Mr. Laurel. Their first impulse was to refuse to form a civilian government on the theory that this was part of a continuing drama to get them. I argued and argued against this view. I wanted to go and talk to Enrile and Ramos about how we could organize a government," said Adaza. "I had always felt that Enrile would someday break away from Marcos. But the problem with our politicians is that they don't study, they don't even read, so very few have a feel for the right meaning of a fast-breaking event."

As more scuttlings in the dark were taking place, the government-controlled television stations looped their videotapes of the Palace coup-plot press conference, playing them over and over again. Radio Veritas tried to balance this by looping its own tapes of the Enrile-Ramos press conference and interviews with the two. At 1:00 A.M., another press conference was held at the Palace. This time, Marcos presented a major who was allegedly one of the assault troops supposed to cross the Pasig River and murder the president. There was still no proof to link Enrile and Ramos to the coup attempt, so would they please stop "this stupidity" and turn in? Enrile went on the air an hour later; he denied the coup plot and said he would talk, why not, but not at the Palace. All through the night, the war of words went on; rebroadcasts of the various press conferences were interspersed—at least on Radio Veritas—with appeals from all kinds of people for help for the Enrile-Ramos faction. Cardinal Sin's appeal seemed to have broken the ice; from minor government functionaries to opposition celebrities, everyone was trying to get into the act on the side of the rebelling soldiers.

The nonattack agreement between Ver and Enrile covered only the camps and the Palace, leaving the church's radio station vulnerable. As the earth turned on its axis, as Saturday, February 22 passed into Sunday, February 23, government troops attacked the Radio Veritas transmitter in Malolos, Bulacan, destroying equipment and causing $2,500,000 worth of damage. Radio Veritas people scurried about for a replacement, turning to the most likely source of help—Fr. James Reuter. An American, long-time resident of Manila, and senior Church Doyen on mass communications, he was overseer of a huge network of print and broadcast production facilities. Father Reuter managed to come up with five alternative stations whose managers agreed to share airtime with Radio Veritas. But the final choice was DZRB, a rather small station that had fallen into disuse. Once owned by the Jacinto family, this, like other Jacinto corporations, had been sequestered in 1972 upon the declaration of martial law. Since then, it had been under military receivership—part of the largesse Marcos shared with the institution he considered his main pillar of support, which this year had also become the primary danger to his regime. Into the tiny station booth went June Keithley, a former host of children's shows suddenly thrust into the middle of a political crisis. She was assured she would be safe since the station was under military control and, although it was far from Camp Aguinaldo, it was still within immediate reach.

Col. Mariano Santiago had gone to Aguinaldo to "commit" his services, with the proviso that he would operate outside the military camps. As he was leaving, he met a Radio Veritas reporter and taped another appeal for people to converge at the camps' area in EDSA. "I then proceeded to Gates One and Two and started to organize the people" clustered there. There were ongoing lectures on how to counter the psychological effect of a possible tank appearance. On a more practical level, the group set to work preparing Molotov cocktails. Around 2:30 A.M., Santiago and an Aquino relative decided to reconnoiter for troop movements. They drove past the Palace, Villamor Airbase, and Fort Bonifacio and noticed nothing unusual. They returned to Camp Aguinaldo, stopping at Gates 3 and 5, again to advise the civilians there on what to do in case tanks showed up. At the AFP Logistics Command, Santiago came across a minor ruckus among students of Ateneo University, a Jesuit institution, and other groups who were manning the gates. To end the dispute, he designated a "man in charge" as head of the group and told them not to allow any vehicle in or out of the compound.

It was already five in the morning by the time he was able to report to General Ramos. Once again, he offered "to tap the tremendous support" that could come "from our civilian populace." Ramos then instructed him to preempt possible artillery deployment at the University of Life compound, which was a project of Mrs. Marcos. Santiago had to go on the air again to call for volunteers.

Danilo Galang left his house early to go to EDSA. He brought along his cameras. He had photographed almost all the major mass actions since the Aquino assassination. He was not about to miss this one. "Life seemed to be going on as usual," he said. But near the road leading to the White Plains subdivision, behind Camp Aguinaldo, he ran into a traffic jam. Vehicles were being rerouted away from EDSA toward White Plains "by a motley group of civilians waving yellow banners on which Benigno Aquino's photograph had been silk-screened," said Galang. He was particularly amused by a young man directing traffic at the intersection. "He had a dark-colored beret on, tilted at a cocky angle, a loose khaki shirt, loose camouflage pants, black and white sneakers, and sunglasses," Galang recalled. "As soon as he saw me aiming my camera, he puffed his chest and started twirling his yellow flag like he was a band major."

That same morning, Monico Atienza and his friend walked to the University of the Philippines, the spawning ground of the anti-Marcos resistance movement. "There were all sorts of emergency meetings by student groups and by the new UP community coalition against fraud and terrorism. A lot of people were confused by what was happening, and the general feeling was that one should be very careful, since the Central Intelligence Agency might be involved in the fracas," Atienza recounted. "By chance, we met a Bayan officer who thought that most cause-oriented groups were stressing a 'preservation-of-forces' approach. But he also said there were already delegations at EDSA and other strategic points." The ambivalence came from a conflict between the immediate emotional response to the rebellion and a cooler rational evaluation of the situation. As Homobono Adaza pointed out, "People went to EDSA out of hatred for the regime, not from love of anyone."

Galang, on foot now, saw that the entire breadth of EDSA had been barricaded with "puny-looking pieces of broken-up concrete that certainly would not stop anything." He walked north toward Boni Serrano Avenue and met a friend who, like him, was into mountain climbing. The friend clapped him on the back, saying that "after this, we can go climb mountains again." There were only a few men and women at Gate 5, and they had formed themselves into a human barricade. "The whole of EDSA was an open stretch of road, with only a few hundreds trudging their way to the Camp Crame front gates and to Camp Aguinaldo's Gate Three." There were no more than twenty thousand people at this point. "I waded through to the gate and took shots of the people who had clambered up the camp walls and the iron gates of Camp Crame. Here a handful of combat troopers stood guard with their assault rifles festooned with yellow ribbons. Overhead, the gate's iron grilles bloomed with the flags and banners of moderate groups," he said.

Southern Luzon's Fr. Jose Dizon was back at EDSA, noting nervously that there were too few civilians in the area. "The people started arriving only around noon," he said. By this time, the U.S. position regarding the revolt—that Marcos should not use U.S.-supplied weapons—had become general knowledge. And much of the confusion was being resolved in favor of an emotional wish to stick one's tongue out at Marcos. Bayan, however, took the precaution of sending former Sen. Lorenzo Tañada to the camp to check out what the whole thing was all about. Labor leader Rolando Olalia, the Nationalist Alliance's Jose Castro, and others of the organizations of the poor had also gone to the camps. Enrile reportedly said he was happy that Bayan people had come, and he assured the former senator that he and his men would recognize Mrs. Aquino's leadership. Tañada then said that Bayan would mobilize.

Salvacion Bueno left her seven children that morning because she heard the appeal over the radio. "They said it was necessary to barricade EDSA," she said, "and so what else was there to do?" She did not worry that after her month's campaign for the Aquino-Laurel ticket, her poll-watching, and all the days she'd spent at the National Assembly, her children would no longer recognize her. She brought the two eldest and left her thirteen-year-old daughter in charge of the rest. She knew this could be a protracted vigil, but "I didn't think of the possibility that I might be killed, or that I might get sick. It was just a necessary thing to do."

Inside the camp, mass was being celebrated by Fr. Joaquin Bernas, rector of Ateneo University, and by the parish priest of a nearby village. The media and what soldiers could be spared from guard duty gathered in the social hall. Even Ramos, a Protestant, attended the mass; Enrile and his men took holy communion. Cardinal Sin later pointed out that, terrified by the thought of death, Enrile had asked for communion while Ramos had held on to a statue of the Virgin Mary. After the mass, the priests asked the defense minister to kneel and, pouring holy water on his head, gave him their blessing.

Ramos, on his way to Camp Crame across the street, was besieged by the crowd. Danilo Galang recalled that the general wore a charcoal-gray bush jacket and matching pants and that he was once again chomping on a cigar, a habit he'd gotten into in hopes that it would help give him a grandson. The rather slight general was hoisted atop an old desk and handed a megaphone. From the improvised stage, he harangued the crowd. "First, he announced the break with Marcos because Marcos did not win the election," said Galang. "Next, he announced receipt of messages of support from abroad and the defections of various military units and commands." Each mention of a unit was met with fervent cheering. "Ramos then appealed to the men and officers of the armed forces to abandon Marcos and Ver since the two could not do what real soldiers were supposed to do: fight, parachute from the air to the ground, and so forth. He was invoking experiences familiar to and shared by the soldiers" to help them make up their minds.

As Ramos spoke, people trekked down EDSA. "The number of people swelled dramatically," Galang said. "They came from all directions—Cubao, Makati, Boni Serrano. Bayan's Waldy Carbonell was directly behind Ramos, waving a Philippine flag." In a matter of minutes, there were a hundred thousand men, women, and children at EDSA, yelling and cheering "all the way" at the general. Following Ramos's speech, Colonel Santiago asked for volunteers to form a people's militia. Most of those who did were members of the League of Filipino Students and the underground youth organization Kabataang Makabayan—though they could not display their banners.

At this point, Galang was assailed by a disturbing thought: "Not a single military unit had been sent out to do reconnaissance," he said. "It occurred to me that the mutinying rebel soldiers were doing their darnedest to prevent a frontal clash between themselves and units still loyal to the regime. And to achieve this and preserve the basic unity of the military, whatever the outcome, they were using civilians as buffers."

Nevertheless, he trudged along with the media people who trailed Ramos back to Camp Crame. There the general gave the media a "hasty tour of the dilapidated offices of the Philippine Constabulary commanding general—which was Ramos, of course. It was to illustrate government neglect of the armed forces. Then he led us to the office of the vice chief of staff, which had become the nerve center of the mutiny. Surprisingly, nothing had been cut off. There was water and electricity; the phones were working. Both sides seemed to have agreed not to inconvenience each other unduly."

The Aquino party was still hammering out its position, and only Adaza seemed to have felt the urgency of the moment. "I had suggested that a committee be formed to negotiate with the defense minister and the general," Adaza recalled, "but nobody would volunteer to go to Camp Aguinaldo. They said there were too many guns there. Finally I volunteered, and so the others had to volunteer. But we still had another meeting in the late afternoon, and by the time we got to Camp Aguinaldo, it was evening. Here I met a newspaper woman on the stairs. She started pulling me away; she was greatly excited. She said Enrile had already called for the formation of a civilian government and we should go to Mrs. Aquino. I told her no; you're not an official representative. We're the official representatives, so we'll speak to the defense minister."

The group and Minister Enrile, according to Adaza, agreed that a provisional coalition government should be set up, based on the 1973 Constitution. The National Assembly should proclaim Mrs. Aquino president. "As soon as Marcos was driven away," Adaza said, "the Cabinet would be expanded. Enrile and Ramos would constitute the military arm of the government; we in the opposition headed by Mrs. Aquino and Mr. Laurel would constitute the civilian government." Despite her suspicions, Mrs. Aquino had already broken her silence in Cebu City, urging the nation to support the rebelling soldiers. She had also asked Marcos to step down so that a peaceful transfer of power could be carried out. Lastly, she had asked government officials to dissociate themselves from the Marcos government.

"At around eleven A.M.," Luis Teodoro said, "I received a call from Becky Patrimonio, assistant to Adrian Cristobal. The 'chairman'—i.e., Cristobal—wanted to meet the leading officers of the President's Center for Special Studies (PCSS) at his Alabang house. Normally the trip would have taken an hour, but since EDSA was blocked, I had to take a roundabout way to the South Expressway. That ate up an hour and a half. There weren't too many vehicles on the roads. There was an armored personnel carrier of the light armored unit of the Philippine Marines in a street off EDSA at the Makati interchange.

"It was around five P.M. when I reached the chairman's house. Dr. Armando Bonifacio, director of the Marcos ideology program; Hazel Gacutan, PCSS deputy director; and others of Mr. Cristobal's circle were there. He asked for our evaluation. Gacutan said the whole revolt was merely an incident, that Ramos and Enrile would be dislodged. Others agreed with him. Mr. Cristobal asked me what I thought, and I said that the fall of the Marcos regime was only a matter of time, that it was suffering from regime fatigue. I also told him about a bit of gossip I'd picked up: that a U.S. embassy official had gathered the heads of multinational corporations in Manila sometime before the election and sounded them out as to Marcos's possible removal. Mr. Cristobal asked why he had not been informed of this. I told him I had passed it on to Mr. Gacutan even though it had seemed like wild rumor to me."

Cristobal kept them until eight o'clock. "He seemed to be trying to decide what to do," Teodoro said. On the way home, he saw "armored trucks and military jeeps filled with soldiers armed to the teeth in the near-empty streets bisecting EDSA near the interchange."

At Malacanang Palace, none of the groundskeepers noticed anything unusual except for the construction of a wooden stage. Marcos, who had toyed with the idea of postponing his inauguration, was now proceeding full speed ahead. It would be held at the Palace on February 25 at noon.

At EDSA, Danilo Galang was beginning to suffer hunger pains. "I estimated the defenders of Camp Aguinaldo to be around three hundred, many of them rear-echelon soldiers who appeared to be lackluster about the whole enterprise." This was a wait-and-see day. The camp gates were still closed, but civilians pressed against the iron grilles, passing enormous quantities of food into the camp. Galang saw soldiers stashing away canned goods, while others toted plastic bags bulging with food back to their quarters.

Cardinal Sin, who'd been told to vacate his archbishop's palace in case Marcos's military came for him, was most touched by a beggar who had heard the cardinal's appeal for food over the radio. The beggar limped over to EDSA and accosted the first soldier he saw. "I'm hungry," the man said, "but you also need food. May I give you the little I have managed to get?"

Salvacion Bueno was trying to shade herself from the hot sun with a piece of cardboard. The flow of people seemed endless. She was not hungry; there was food being passed around from hand to hand, brought over by nuns. After a while, she joined in the food distribution, handing out to the crowd boiled eggs, juice in Styrofoam cups, and odds and ends of donated edibles.

Toti arrived that noon. He had not told his mother he was going to EDSA, letting her believe he would be at his usual post at the Katipunan-Aurora Boulevard intersection. He did go there, he said, as if to assuage the guilt of this un-filial conduct. But the usual crowd of cigarette boys had dwindled to two or three, all of whom were planning to go to EDSA. Toti hung fire, thinking that if his competitors left, he could hog the cigarette trade the whole day. But as the hours passed and the asphalt burned through the thin soles of his rubber slippers and carbon monoxide filled his lungs, restlessness descended upon him. He tried to still it, telling himself that Alicia, who was younger, was yet re-sponsible enough to have taken her supply of flower gar-lands from the wholesale man and to have left for her hawking post without a murmur. He could do no less, he thought, jamming on the ragged baseball cap he wore with its beak to the back.

But it was a losing fight. Curiosity mounted steadily, and finally he edged farther and farther away from the cor-ner, studiously selling cigarettes all the while. "*Yosi*, boss?"

It was a dangerous thing to do; he could have gotten beaten up, since each group of cigarette vendors had their territory. That was preordained, he said. He would not elaborate.

Willy-nilly, he was pulled toward EDSA; as if doing penance, he walked all the way. He could feel himself burning black in the sun. He had a bottle of Coke at Cubao, and that was delicious, but lunch he eschewed. As he neared EDSA, he sniffed a change in the wind. "You can smell people a mile away," he said, "and I knew this was a large one." Closer still, he could hear the noise—a dull roar, as of some beast, overwhelming traffic sounds. He broke into a run, hit the crowd's edge in a sprint, and wedged his way through. He'd forgotten his trade and remembered with a start only when he saw the parked vendor carts with their boiled corn, peanuts, eggs, soda pop. But since he wanted to see what was going on, what held the crowd to-gether, he went on wending his way toward the camp gate.

There were so many priests and nuns, he said, even more than he'd seen at the convent school near his selling post. He looked at the nuns intently, wondering as other children did whether their headdresses covered extremely short or normal-length hair. Near the gate, he was hailed by a well-dressed man who asked how much his entire stock was. Toti, round-eyed, told him, and the man started counting bills into his pack, added another twenty-peso bill for the box. Then he carted the whole thing off. "He shoved it through the iron bars of the gate," Toti said, "for the sol-diers."

Each lane of EDSA, according to Galang, "was a virtual sea of people." He spotted a woman distributing food inside Camp Crame and begged for a share. But then he had to bolt down the boiled egg and juice he received because a strange sight had appeared: a combat trooper, as impassive as Rambo, wearing a Rambo headband of olive drab strips with the ends trailing to his shoulders. Although he had an M-16 in his right hand and an M-79 slung across his back, he was cradling a two-foot statue of the Virgin Mary in the crook of his left arm.

Shortly thereafter, pandemonium broke out: "*Mga kaaway* ('the enemy')!" The shouts ricocheted through the crowd. Galang saw how quickly even a jam-packed crowd could move. Media people scampered for cover; video crews and photographers clambered for vantage points. Nearby soldiers cocked and aimed their guns. "It turned out that several fire trucks and lorries of crowd control troops had arrived at Pedro Tuazon street, a kilometer to the north. They had been ordered by the Palace to disperse the human barricades protecting the two camps," Galang said.

But as he looked in the northern direction, he saw that that stretch of EDSA was a solid mass of people. The Boni Serrano–EDSA intersection was barricaded with buses and bags of concrete and stone. "The troops, not having received any orders to disembark, stayed aboard the lorries. There were about 300 to 350 of them; plus maybe about ten policemen," Galang said.

"Together with Butz Aquino and thousands of people," Colonel Santiago recounted, "I approached the antiriot army men. Butz talked to General Alfredo Lim of the Northern Police District." Santiago himself, accompanied by two Philippine Military Academy cadets, talked to the uniformed men. "I asked them to look around, look at the size of the crowd giving its all for a united stand for a change in government leadership."

The crowd made pleading noises at the soldiers; hands flashed the L sign. Galang watched as the civilians offered the troops food, drink, and cigarettes. "Some clambered aboard the lorries and embraced the soldiers," he said. A few soldiers smiled; most looked bewildered. "The people persisted." A newsboy offered a soldier a newspaper so he could "bone up on fast-breaking events." In the end, they could not carry out their mission. Marcos later berated General Lim, saying, "You have failed me. I ordered you to disperse the crowd!"

At three o'clock, Enrile, who had fallen asleep, was awakened by an aide. It had been decided that Camp Crame was easier to defend and that the forces of the two leaders of the revolt should be consolidated. Picking up his Uzi, Enrile prepared to move out, hemmed in on all sides by his security detail. In such a crowd, a knife would be a quick and efficient weapon. At Gate 1, though, the minister caught his first glimpse of the throng. That was enough to cause him to blurt out "Oh, my God!" An honor guard of nuns waving rosaries and the image of the Virgin escorted him across EDSA as the crowd broke into cheers, into hand-waving, into applause, into screams of approbation. A forest of hands proffered rosaries, thrusting them into Enrile's pockets, winding them about his neck. Charlyn Zlotnick, carrying her camera, had to walk backward all the way from Camp Aguinaldo to Crame, holding the minister in the center of her lens.

Bishop Antonio Nepomuceno, who had rushed to Manila from Mindanao upon hearing of the mutiny, was in Camp Crame, along with other media people waiting for yet another press conference. "We stood around waiting and waiting," the bishop said. "Finally a soldier came and said they had just received an ultimatum, and the camps were going to be shelled. Well, we said, we'll just stay here. But then the sound of a helicopter came, and everybody ran out. The press conference was scuttled." Meanwhile, as he was walking toward Camp Crame, Galang saw a woman holding out a baby no more than two months old to a hole in the camp fence. A hand reached out of the hole and caressed the baby briefly. It was the father—a soldier who could not go off-duty at this tense hour.

Inside the camp, Galang caught sight of a platoon of irregulars who kept by themselves. There was an Aeta (an aborigine) with them. His curiosity pricked, Galang approached the group. Since the group spoke Ilocano, he did too. "The unit came all the way from Gattaran, Cagayan," he said. "There were sixty of them, and they had been in Manila since Thursday to serve as the minister's security, they said. The platoon leader suddenly interjected that actually the group were NPAs—New People's Army members."

Further questioning ferreted out the truth. The group were either NPAs who had surrendered or deep-penetration agents who could no longer maintain their cover. Nevertheless, they were still going around presenting themselves as NPAs. "I asked who their commanding officer was," Galang said, and when the men looked toward a direction, Galang followed their eyes. He nodded to himself. "Just as I suspected. It was Col. Rodolfo Aguinaldo—a most unconventional and notorious military officer. He stood at parade rest with his Israeli Galil assault rifle, the mark of the Ministry of National Defense Security Group."

Romeo Candazo of Selda (Prison Cell), the organization of former political prisoners, said that although the central leadership of most cause-oriented groups remained hesitant, their local chapters had taken the initiative. "In Sta. Mesa, chapter members brought down all the trees along the roads leading to the Palace, while University of the Philippines members went straight to EDSA. Everyone responded in whatever form and way they were capable of. But you have to appreciate the dilemma of our people. They went to EDSA only to be confronted by the faces of those who tortured them. It was a heavy trip. Nevertheless, they stayed."

Toti spent his time ogling the soldiers, wondering when he could have a pair of camouflage pants. There were hordes of children in the crowd; almost all the street kids in the vicinity were there. "I don't know why, but we seem to know everything that goes on," Toti said, scratching his head. His cigarettes had sold out and food was plentiful, so he was content to stay where he was. But turning toward the southern end of the crowd, he found his sister playing with other girls who were as wild looking as she was. "He rapped me on the head," Alicia said. The two exchanged curses, scandalizing some nuns. Alicia had sold her flowers, and many of the Virgin Mary and Christ Child statues were garlanded with her wares. She stuck her tongue out at her brother and ran away; she said later that she had also had her "revolution."

Suddenly, news of a marine contingent rumbling down EDSA flashed over the transistor radios that the crowd had brought along. This was no joke, friend; these were armed personnel carriers and tanks. Tanks! Everybody had been waiting for tanks, and here they were, rolling down from Fort Bonifacio, headed by the marine commandant himself, Gen. Artemio Tadiar. Enrile picked up the phone and made two calls, one to U.S. Ambassador Bosworth, the other to General Ver. He told the first that there were seven tanks and two battalions to the south and a tank column to the north. There were hundreds of media people, said Enrile, in the defense ministry, Americans among them. He said the same thing to Ver, adding that Ver and Marcos would go down in history as "butchers of your own officers and men, of the Filipino people and foreign mediamen." Ver promised to tell his men not to push the civilians.

Toti, running with the crowd, caught sight of his first tank: "It was *big!*" He'd never felt as small in his entire life, and in a fit of helplessness he clutched at the shoulder of the woman before him. The intersection had been barricaded with five buses and chunks of concrete that the panicked crowd had torn off the road surface with their bare hands. "But it was so *big!*" Toti kept saying.

Then the armored personnel carriers came into view, and a shudder went through the crowd. Those in the front lines fell to their knees, and in the sudden hush a clear female voice tolled the words of the prayer to the Virgin Mary. Only then did Toti realize that he could hold the woman's shoulder because she was down, kneeling or sitting, and he was the only one standing. Then voices took up the response to the prayer; the words fell as lightly as the breeze that came down the road. Men and women had shut their eyes, and tears were rolling down their faces; they refused even to acknowledge the danger before them.

In another section of the road, women broke from the crowd and surrounded the armored personnel carriers and tanks. They clambered all over the vehicles and tried to push them back with their bare hands, or they proffered flowers, rosaries, and candies to the bemused soldiers. Gen. Artemio Tadiar found himself besieged by calls of "Temy! Temy!" Strange voices crooned his nickname like a song. Tadiar gave the crowd thirty minutes to clear the road and remove the barricades. But he and the soldiers were surrounded by women—nuns and laity—who begged, pleaded, prayed, and patted their shoulders and backs soothingly.

Agapito "Butz" Aquino had clambered atop one of the tanks; he nearly fell off when it rumbled. The tanks turned abruptly and rolled away, and the carriers did a right face and rumbled into a vacant lot. The crowd screamed joy at its deliverance. Toti blew his nose on his T-shirt.

Enrile later said that perhaps it was because of his talk with Ver that Tadiar's unit was asked not to fire. But Cardinal Sin also said that after the commotion a group of soldiers had come to him asking to see the beautiful sister who had stopped them from shooting at the people. He didn't want to start a rumor, the cardinal said, so he merely told the soldiers that the nuns were elsewhere. "But I believe it was the Lady herself," he said.

As the marines maintained a strict rectangular defense perimeter in the vacant lot, said Galang, the crowd pressed in on them. He counted three battalions all in all, led by four sixty-ton Korean War–vintage amphibious assault vehicles. There was also a squadron of light armored vehicles known as Chemites, or V15s. "General Artemio Tadiar himself commanded the marines," Galang said, "and nearly all the officers around him seemed short-fused. A major kept snarling at media people crossing the defense perimeter. Along EDSA, though, pretty mestiza girls offered flowers to battle-hardened marines; kneeling nuns were still praying the rosary, while seminarians kept raising their crosses to the marines' faces [as if] they were *conquistadores* confronting heathens." Sister Bobbie of St. Scholastica College wandered among the soldiers, blessing them and murmuring, "Peace be with you, brothers."

Santiago walked to his erstwhile colleagues, and there, hearing the officers speak for the first time, he "became quite emotional," he admitted. The officers were convinced that Enrile's group had attempted a coup. They had themselves caught some of the plotters, including a Captain Aspisin, who were "trying to probe the defense of the marines at Fort Bonifacio during a night run." One officer was sure that Mrs. Aquino's camp had cheated in the election because he had been prevented from voting by a NAMFREL volunteer, despite a COMELEC ruling that soldiers could vote at precincts near their assigned posts. Somewhat dazed, suddenly feeling his ties with the troops, Santiago turned away.

This first attempt to breach his civilian defense broke down Enrile's reluctance to speak to Marcos. Cagayan's assemblyman had been nudging the defense minister to make that phone call, and now Enrile reluctantly agreed. He said hello; Marcos said hello. The president invited his rebellious soldiers to surrender. He really had no intention of punishing Enrile's men, though they would have to go through a pro forma trial "to show the public that we enforce the law"—after which Marcos would pardon them all. Enrile replied by saying he didn't know how his men would react to that, and he would discuss the offer with them.

That evening, the opposition leaders arrived. "They and Minister Enrile met at the conference hall," said Colonel Isleta. No one said what was discussed. Enrile claimed later that he had urged the leaders to form a civilian government so he and his men could be freed to concentrate on the military aspects of the revolt. After the conference, Enrile sent a presidential emissary back to Marcos, with the message that there was no going around it; his group's "irreducible" demand was that the president step down.

Late in the evening, Danilo Galang left EDSA by a circuitous route. The road was already impassable. He arrived home in time to catch a live television broadcast from the Palace. Marcos shrieked that Enrile and the RAM officers were the coup plot masterminds. As he spoke, the noise of hammering resounded in the background as the inaugural stage was rushed to completion. There would be no grand bash this time at Rizal Park. Still, Marcos vowed to crush the revolt.

Shortly after that, intelligence reports reached the camps that an attack would be launched early Monday morning. The situation did not look good for the rebels. There were tanks at Cubao, marines within Camp Aguinaldo, commandos at Horseshoe Boulevard, tanks at EDSA, and mortars at Greenhills. In brief, they were surrounded not only by people but also by Marcos forces. But the crowd outside, among them Salvacion Bueno, Toti, Alicia, and other nameless but at this instant powerful men and women, lay propped up against walls, curled on pieces of cardboard and on newspaper sheets, and slept the sleep of the just.

NINE

The Balance Tilts

At two o'clock on Monday morning, February 24, the tense stillness at EDSA remained unbroken. In the operational headquarters of Gen. Fidel Ramos, the phone lines hummed, typewriters banged, and bursts of static came from walkie-talkies. Everyone waited for the gunfire that would signal the expected attack. Just before midnight His Excellency, President Ferdinand E. Marcos, had ordered on television the "crushing" of the rebellion. At two-thirty, Colonel Isleta looked up and told Ramos that he didn't think the attack would push through; it was a half hour late already. Ramos nodded but went on working.

An hour later, the night stirred. Trucks full of soldiers arrived; they formed ranks and eyeballed the crowd at Santolan Road. But the men and women, jolted from sleep, linked arms and refused to budge. Seminarians raised their crosses; women, their rosaries. From behind the soldiers came voices urging them, "Advance! Advance!" A student felt his hair stand up and, wishing to be reassured, glanced at the woman to his right, whose arm was entwined with his. "She was white-haired and all of ninety pounds, maybe," he said. He glanced to his left and saw a fifteen-year-old girl. "I just closed my eyes—*bahala na* ('What will be, will be')," he said, and strangely enough felt strength and comfort flow through him from the arms pressing against his and from the body heat that surrounded him. From nearby houses, other voices rang out, appealing to the soldiers, "*Totoy, totoy* ('son')!" They were old women's voices and quavering old men's voices. The soldier's line wavered. Then tear-gas canisters arched forward, fell to the road, and burst. White mist rose rapidly, enwrapping the human barricade. Now the wall of human bodies crumbled as coughing fits echoed down the line and tears squeezed out of their eyes. "Nobody moves!" a female voice screamed. The student thought his arms would break, so rigidly did he hold on to the others. Suddenly the wind shifted. The gas blew toward the soldiers. The two lines of massed bodies, each weeping, confronted each other. "Fix bayonets!" came the order. The blades glinted. A tremor ran through the crowd; it reared back and then held. "It was too much," a soldier said later. "We were thoroughly disheartened. The thought of ramming bayonets through those bodies—it was just too sickening."

At Ortigas-EDSA, the rumble of tanks was heard again. Its defenders, a motley group of students and ordinary men and women, held their breath. Then the silhouette of two tanks pierced the dim light of streetlamps. The crowd hissed; the tanks came on, reached the outer edge of the barricade, stopped, hesitated, and turned around. A scream of joy ripped through the night air, but it was hushed just as suddenly when two armored personal carriers hovered into sight. A mumble of prayers rose again, an exorcism of the devil's spawn. The APCs came on, almost kissed the first human barricade, stopped, hesitated, and turned around. Cheers once more. "It was getting to be boring," said a young man, "this dance of tanks and APCs."

Unknown to the street defenders, the buildings surrounding Camp Crame had been seeded with rebel snipers,

and in private residences the manufacture of Molotov cocktails was going on relentlessly; soutaned seminarians over-
saw some of those instant production lines. Firearms had
also been distributed—discreetly, mostly to "the well-
heeled," said Galang. Peaceful was peaceful as could be, but
no one was going down without causing Marcos maximum
damage.

So far, the furor had been largely concentrated in
Metro-Manila, between Malacanang Palace by the Pasig
River in the heart of the city proper and Camps Aguinaldo
and Crame on Epifanio de los Santos Avenue in the center
of Quezon City, the official capital of the nation. But the rest
of the country was not about to let Manilans steal the show.
From Central Mindanao, a battalion of combat soldiers hi-
jacked a Philippine Airlines DC-10 and landed at the Manila airport, only to walk straight into a ring of tanks. They
were disarmed and brought to Fort Bonifacio. From Min-
doro, a ship chartered by approximately three hundred
Bayan members came to augment the EDSA crowd. From
north, south, east, and west, by whatever means they could
manage, Filipinos were marching to the city. Those who
couldn't began barricading highways in anticipation of
tanks and troops from provincial military forts. Because the
armed forces, set up in 1903 by the U.S. colonial government, were intended for internal pacification, it was largely
a land force rather than air and naval power better suited to
the archipelago. The people acted accordingly. As far north
as the Aquinos' home province, Tarlac, and as far south as
Bicol, the national highway was segmented by groups of
men and women keeping vigil, waiting for Marcos's tanks.

At 5:00 A.M., General Ramos looked up and said that a
rocket attack was on the way. Everyone not involved with
operations would have to go downstairs. For the first time,
Colonel Isleta grew conscious of danger and had an unchar-
itable thought. "There I was, with no weapon, not even a
flak jacket," he said. "I went to an officer and asked if any
M-16s were left. But he said everything had been issued
out. I went back to the room and looked around. I saw the

soldier standing beside the door. And I thought, if anything happens, he will be the first to get it. In which case, I will grab his weapon."

By this time, the Palace itself was ringed by a crowd, mostly of members of the labor federation, the KMU, and the League of Filipino Students, but also of individuals from the nearby communities. It was no surprise that they formed the bulk of the crowd here. Ironically, the Palace was located in the midst of lower-middle- and working-class residential districts that had watched in silent resentment the beautification of the presidential grounds while their own communities sank into a morass of uncollected garbage, decaying structures, and seasonal floods. As for the students, the Palace had been their traditional protest area. It was a mere half-mile from University Belt, a stretch of downtown Manila where school buildings stood nearly shoulder to shoulder.

Fr. Jose Dizon had been standing with the EDSA crowd for hours now and was getting impatient. "Enrile and Ramos obviously weren't going to move; they were waiting for Marcos to resign. Now, how could that happen without a direct threat on his life? We decided we'd better move to the seat of power—Malacanang Palace—and make a feint at it." So Bayan members began massing at Nagtahan and Laurel streets, joining neighborhood residents who were already there. "There were tanks and people all over the place. I looked the crowd over and estimated we were twenty-five thousand strong."

At EDSA, Monico Atienza said, the crowd had lost its middle-class character and was now diluted with legions of workers, squatter area residents, and urban poor—the great unwashed. Although there was some resentment at their presence, they could not be driven away. They provided the mass necessary to keep the rebellion's leadership viable. Cause-oriented groups had also broken out their banners and had occupied strategic spots in EDSA, in Santolan Road, in the Cubao district, and in Bohol Avenue, as well as in the intersection of streets leading to the Palace. Like night flowers, the banners flapped in the wind: KASAPI, BANDILA, ATOM, BAYAN, NATIONALIST ALLIANCE, GABRIELA.

Luis Teodoro was awakened at dawn by his phone ringing. It was a friend who, although virulently anti-Marcos, had managed to retain his sources of information within the government. "Leave the University campus," the friend said. "It will be sealed off by Marcos troops." The previous evening, he said, the Palace circle had decided to go all out on Monday morning. Troops would storm Camp Aguinaldo, disperse the crowd, and engage the Ramos-Enrile forces in a total war. Marines were already positioning artillery and mortar pieces to pound Camp Crame. After the mutiny's defeat, the regime would declare martial law and arrest or liquidate opposition leaders, cause-oriented organization leaders, and all former political prisoners. At this news Teodoro, who'd spent seven months in jail, raised his eyebrows, dropped the phone, and moved his entire household to his mother's residence.

Colonel Santiago was back at EDSA at six that morning with one thought firm in his mind: Action had to be taken; the stalemate had lasted too long. Hearing of the attempt to disperse the crowd at Santolan Road, he realized it was only a matter of time before Marcos's troops reached Ramos and Enrile. He felt he had to "open a new front" to ease the pressure on the two camps. Channel 4, a government television station, seemed the logical target. He had loaded up on empty bottles and gasoline for Molotov cocktails—donations from a gas station owner. He knew he was going to go for Channel 4.

As soon as he arrived, he asked for volunteers. A young woman who was hefting a megaphone countered that this action would go against Mrs. Aquino's policy of nonviolence, and she urged the crowd not to join. Santiago, losing his temper, grabbed the megaphone from her and let loose with an explanation of the whys and wherefores of his plan. At that moment, about two hundred members of ATOM-Bayan, their banner aloft, were marching toward EDSA from Santolan. Santiago approached their leader and asked that the group join the expedition to Channel 4. They agreed. All in all, about a thousand people marched with Santiago, including Salvacion Bueno, who had not left EDSA at all.

As the group left for the target station, six Sikorsky helicopters winged toward Camp Crame. The crowd lifted its eyes to the sky, saw the rocket turrets of the aircraft, and quivered. A terrible hush blanketed the crowd. Some ducked, sprawling on the street; others gripped rosaries and began the Lord's Prayer. The few who held statues of the Virgin and the Christ Child tightened their grip on them.

Toti, who'd breakfasted well for the first time in his life, had been about to sneak off to a corner of the camp's wall to pee when the helicopters appeared. He saw them circle, then swoop down; he heard the women scream, "They're going to strafe, they're going to strafe, down, down, *dapa!*" Prayers again. *Into thy hands I commend my spirit.* In the aircraft, the commanding officer, Col. Antonio Sotelo, who'd been ordered to fire at Camp Crame as soon as the crowd dispersed, was saying his own prayer, asking for guidance. The crowd held, packed tighter than sardines; they were a certain sacrifice.

Then the helicopters landed. The first soldier the crowd glimpsed was Sotelo, who was flashing the L sign. Colonel Isleta, still in the operations room, watched the door open and Sotelo walk in. The colonel saluted Ramos and said, "Sir, your air force is here." The Fifteenth Strike Wing had defected. Downstairs, the crowd found its way into the camp and was embracing the soldiers. Toti touched the helicopters with reverence; he had not even dreamed he would ever be that close to an aircraft.

Alicia, his sister, was more pragmatic. After separating from Toti, she had found herself a congenial niche near a nuns' food-distribution center. She was busy helping gather trash and refuse, stashing it into plastic bags. It was household work, she said, and—as usual—women had to do it.

That early morning, Eubolio Verzosa, vice president of

the Channel 7 corporation, was awakened by a different kind of problem. His newsroom was trying to get in touch with him; they were preparing a news bulletin that Marcos had already left the country. Verzosa grabbed his walkie-talkie and asked his men to verify the information. But the head of the newsroom said the story had come over the wires of the Philippine News Agency, which was government owned. "Our Malacanang reporter had already gone out to check. He reported that the Palace was unusually quiet," Verzosa said. "The troops there were all wearing white armbands—which he said General Ramos took to be a signal of surrender." So Channel 7 broadcast the news that Marcos and his family had left the Palace.

On hearing this news, the crowd at EDSA gave a celebratory roar and, weeping and jumping, embraced one another as well as whatever soldiers they could lay their hands on. "Enrile and Ramos appeared," recalled Danilo Galang, "before a sizable gathering at the Philippine Constabulary headquarters. Ramos announced more defections to their side, including navy combat ships. He sounded as though the tide was steadily turning in favor of the mutiny. Enrile spoke next, and this time he no longer looked worried and scared. He was stern and cocky. Almost immediately, he went into a tirade against Communists and the New People's Army, warning them of dire consequences should they take advantage of the situation. I took this to be a signal to the U.S., that it was back to business as usual."

The two then proceeded to EDSA, where they addressed nearly 500,000 people massed along the road. Here, General Ramos gave the little leap of joy immortalized by many a camera. "I managed to get a shot of Enrile crying," Galang said, "as he was being shepherded through the throng which was chanting his name: 'Johnny! Johnny!' " But as the gates of Camp Crame opened and the crowd surged in, two F-5 fighter planes arrived. "They started to buzz the camp, flying in ever-descending circles. This went on for about thirty minutes while the crowd watched. I was afraid they would start to strafe. Then to my relief the planes flew away."

In a maximum security cell, Bernabe Buscayno found the situation well-nigh intolerable. He could hear the roar of the crowd outside and caught bits and pieces of what was going on from his guards. But having practically grown up with a gun in his hand, he felt helpless. "I would get excited, hearing the people shouting and cheering," he later said. "Then I'd realize where I was and how possible it was to get killed just like that—I'd get depressed."

Near Channel 4, Colonel Santiago stopped his rag-tag army at the last intersection before the television compound. He turned over command of "people power" to Capt. Juan Vicente Resurreccion, whom they'd met along the way. The few soldiers with the crowd had only sidearms; the crowd, of course, was unarmed. But this did not bother Santiago, who formed a negotiating team and proceeded to the station. The first two soldiers they met refused to talk, but at the entrance a guard told him that the compound was secured by Aviation Security Command (AVSECOM) rangers. This was not good news; AVSECOM was under Col. Luther Custodio and had been implicated in Aquino's assassination. (The Aquino-Galman murder case has been reopened and the Philippine Supreme Court is reviewing testimony against General Fabian Ver and 25 others.)

Santiago asked that people be deployed at various exits of the television compound. Then, using a megaphone, he asked for Lt. Col. Ruben Ronas, the commanding officer. "He happened to have been my colleague at the Presidential Security Command," he later said. When Ronas appeared, Santiago asked him to turn over the station peacefully to avoid bloodshed. Ronas asked for time to contact Information Minister Greg Cendaña. Santiago gave him thirty minutes, during which time some of the men and women who'd marched with him asked to use the megaphone. They knew employees inside the compound and wanted to appeal to them to come out and join the people. A few responded and abandoned Channel 4.

When the deadline arrived, Santiago called to Ronas, who asked for more time. He was about to give the man another deadline when news of reinforcements from Camp Crame came. Despite this, Ronas could not make up his mind. "Four cars of the Constabulary Highway Patrol Group arrived, and I told Ronas that they were here, that I could not guarantee his safety anymore, and that it might be our last meeting." The officer paled and said *"Huwag naman* ('Please don't'), sir." Then another contingent from the Constabulary Narcotics Command came, and Santiago had fifty armed men behind him.

Small explosions told Santiago that the soldiers were trying to sabotage the transmitters. His men rushed forward to open the main gate but were met with gunfire. For about ten minutes bullets raked the air; then Santiago called for a cease-fire. But in the sudden lull, a young member of ATOM rushed to the station, clambered up the flagpole, and hoisted a yellow banner. Everybody cheered and applauded, thinking the station had fallen. Apparently, so did the troops inside. Seven Marcos soldiers came out bearing a wounded colleague and surrendered. Then two more, carrying a dead soldier.

Reinforcements from the Marcos camp, though, were rushing toward Channel 4. The first to arrive were SWAT teams from the police. But the armored personnel carriers and truckloads of soldiers that had been drawn from provincial commands found the city streets to be alien topography. From time to time, they had to stop and ask street people for directions to the television station. Even flower garland vendors pointed the soldiers anywhere but toward the right location. Eventually the APCs found their way to the station, and gunfire erupted again. Salvacion Bueno, still with the crowd, cowered with the rest.

"We would move forward whenever the guns stopped," she said. "Then they'd go off again and we'd retreat. I was wedged tight between people and had to move every time they moved. For cover, we'd turn our backs to the soldiers and squat. I tucked my head in between my knees and thought that even if I got hit, I'd get it in the ass, not the head—so never mind."

Bishop Nepomuceno, still lugging his video camera, couldn't tell "for the life of me" which were the Marcos troops and which were the rebels. "I was with a group near the loyalist front, I think," he said. "I saw these policemen, and I went up to the leader and asked why they wouldn't go up to this building so they could hit the Marcos soldiers." They turned out to be Marcos men; the bishop hurriedly lost himself in the crowd. The fighting went on for about an hour until a seminarian edged his way to Santiago and said that the commanding officer of the Marcos troops wanted to parlay.

Santiago was shielded by a phalanx of civilians as he walked over to meet the officer. "When I shook his hand, the crowd started clapping," he said. "And I told him it was useless to fight, as we had secured Channel 4 already. I was bluffing." As the two spoke, men and women breached the soldier's ranks, spoke to them, and offered them food. "They forgot about feeding us," said Santiago. "They were feeding the loyalists!" By 3:00 P.M., Santiago was on the air, "live, announcing we were in control of the government television station." It was just in time because Radio Veritas, which had been hit again by Marcos soldiers, had faded. Its personnel moved quickly to Channel 4, waving Vatican flags and singing church hymns along the way.

Fate was not as kind to Channel 7. An hour after broadcasting news of the president's departure, Marcos was back denouncing the misinformation. "I will hold Channel 7 responsible for that announcement," he intoned. Eubolio Verzosa was eating lunch when some of his employees came to tell him that troops had arrived. "Surprisingly, I was very calm," he recalled. "Being the highest official around, I owed it to my people not to show any fear. Of course, my guts were in a different state.

"I asked the commanding officer—a first lieutenant—why he and his men were here. Apparently, they had not been in Manila for long; they came from outside. He said he was told to secure Channel 7; I told him we had not asked for any security. Then I asked him who his commanding officer was so I could verify the order. In the first place, I didn't know what his loyalties were. But he said he wasn't allowed to say even that. To his credit, he was quite apologetic, saying they were just following orders."

The troops—around forty—entered, and Verzosa asked the lieutenant to take his men downstairs. "At that moment, a strange thing happened," he said. "My phone rang." It was Colonel Isleta, saying, "Bobby, I'm sending a contingent there." Verzosa answered nervously, "Nes, don't do that. You will turn our station into a battleground. The Marcos troops are already here." Isleta said okay, but that he was sending people power anyway. "Within ten minutes, the entire area was surrounded by a crowd," Verzosa said.

Now Verzosa gathered his own people and told the engineers to disable the transmitters if the soldiers demanded that they leave. "We did not want our facilities to be used by either side for propaganda," he explained. "We were still broadcasting our regular programs, but after two hours, sure enough, the officer received instructions to have us vacate the premises." They stopped transmission and gathered at the lobby. "We were in full force, around two hundred men and women, and we wanted to leave honorably. We had always maintained our neutrality, that we were true journalists and broadcasters. We resented the troops' telling us to stop broadcasting and leave the compound. It was two-thirty P.M.; we said our prayers in the lobby and sang religious songs. Then we went out and joined the crowd gathered in the streets."

At Malacanang Palace, the first barricades at Mendiola Street—steel trestles festooned with barbed wire—had been stripped clean. For fourteen years, since the declaration of martial law, those trestles had stood there, inviolate and forbidding. Now they were naked. The mostly male crowd wove crowns of barbed wire, the ultimate symbol of the Marcos era. "There was no fiesta-like atmosphere here," said Danilo Galang, who along with two friends had driven to the area. "There was tension and an air of expectation." The calm was broken by the appearance of helicopters that hovered and circled over the compound. Suddenly one swooped down and fired its rockets, hitting the garden of the president's mother.

Those inside the Palace, including Rita Gadi Balthazar, threw themselves down, crawled under tables, or cowered in the toilets. The Marcos women were hysterical. But Enrile had ordered the helicopters to miss the president's residence deliberately—noblesse oblige. The attack apparently convinced many that the Palace wasn't a nice place to be, and the exodus of Marcos's high-powered supporters began. But most nervous were the presidential pilots whose helicopters were parked within the Palace compound and so were sitting ducks; they had been hit by shrapnel.

At Villamor Air Base, three helicopters from Camp Crame suddenly appeared and destroyed five Huey helicopters with rockets. Then they headed for Clark Air Force Base to refuel. According to his senior military aide, Enrile had to beg U.S. base officers for fuel and even offered to pay for it with his personal check.

By the time Bishop Nepomuceno reached Nagtahan, near the Palace, Marcos's troops had massed and "were gearing to come out." The crowd taunted them, daring them to cross the open road.

Overseas, Filipinos in the diplomatic service were resigning throughout the day, urging Marcos to step down. From Honolulu, San Francisco, Houston, and London came news of the defections of ambassadors and consuls. Philippine Airlines suddenly switched to the Aquino camp. Mrs. Marcos's brother, Eduardo "Kokoy" Romualdez, abruptly disappeared with his family. But what really riled up President Marcos was a message from his old-time friend and ally, Adrian Cristobal. "I had the TV set tuned in to Channel 4," said Teodoro, "which had become everyone's favorite station after it fell to rebel hands. It was over this channel that I heard 'the chairman' say that the regime had fallen and that Marcos should heed the people's demand that he step down."

Monday evening in Manila was Sunday morning in the United States, and for once the U.S. president could not observe the no-work-over-the-weekend rule. In a conference with Philip Habib, Defense Secretary Caspar Weinberger, Undersecretary of State Michael Armacost, and the deputy director of the Central Intelligence Agency, Ronald Reagan pondered the fate of his erstwhile friend. It was obvious that, win or lose, Marcos would no longer be able to govern to Philippines. The situation could only worsen. The U.S. president insisted that Marcos must receive better treatment than that which had been afforded the Shah of Iran when he fell from power. That afternoon, Habib gave the National Security Council the same stark briefing: "The Marcos era has ended. He's had it." But it was evening before Armacost could contact Assemblyman Blas Ople, whom Marcos had sent to Washington to "explain" his side of the election issue. Unless Marcos stepped down, Armacost told Ople, the Philippines would slide into a civil war.

Arturo Tolentino sent his own message to Marcos. He wrote that he would not be able to attend the inauguration, scheduled for the following day. However, he was willing to mediate between the president and the Enrile-Ramos faction. Although an earlier letter hadn't made it through the Palace cordon, this one, Tolentino's courier reported, got through.

By early evening, Reagan's new position had hit the airwaves in Manila, evoking a huge hurrah. "Attempts to prolong the life of the current regime are futile. A solution to this crisis can only be achieved through a peaceful transition to a new government." By luck, Ople managed a phone connection to the Palace and gave Marcos the message from Armacost. The president frothed at the mouth: he was being hamstrung; he couldn't use force, and Mrs. Marcos didn't want to leave the Palace.

Two hours later, he was before television cameras again, waging an imaginary war. "I was watching Channel 9, which was still under government control," Teodoro said, "and there was Marcos denying everything. He claimed Adrian Cristobal was with him at the Palace—which tipped me off that he was lying. I knew 'the chairman' did not want to go to the Palace, because he was afraid the military men around Marcos would detain everybody. Anyway, Marcos said Cristobal could not have said what Channel 4 had said he had said." If nothing else, Marcos was well versed in the poker bluff; poker was a favorite game in the Palace, where the antes could be briefcases stuffed with money. Marcos said he was like an old warhorse who grew excited at the smell of gunpowder, that he himself would lead his forces in crushing the rebellion, that he had his own sniper rifle out just in case. He was still in full control of the situation, he said, his voice rasping and wavering in volume.

And then he showed off the generals who remained with him. At this point, General Ver, grim-faced, jumped up and interrupted the presidential harangue. He wanted permission to use artillery to crush the rebellion; he wanted to be allowed to use all-out force. Marcos demurred, saying his men should confine themselves to light weapons; he didn't want people hurt. But the seething general, who obviously was unaware of the U.S. injunction against military force, insisted—and a bone-chilling argument took place in full view of the archipelago: to bomb or not to bomb, to bombard or not to bombard.

But Marcos seemed more worried about the U.S. threat than about the breakdown of his government. A friend theorized that Marcos must have been concerned about all the real estate and money he'd stashed away. "Which goes to show," he said, "that when the chips are down, wealth can become a liability."

Marcos ended his broadcast with a dusk-to-dawn curfew, which set Danilo Galang and his friends, who were having dinner, howling with derision. Luis Teodoro drove toward EDSA and found that the crowd had spilled over to the Cubao junction, "meaning that a two-kilometer stretch of bodies protected the camps. Channel 4 was also ringed by people. People were in a festive mood; hawkers were having a field day, selling cigarettes, peanuts, soda, and yellow ribbons. Entire families were camped out, with food and chairs and mats." Because Marcos had said they should not be out, everybody decided it was a good occasion to take the night air. The streets near the contested areas—Channel 4, the Palace, and EDSA—were illuminated by flames from burning car tires. White-soutaned seminarians directed the strengthening of barricades. Meanwhile, the beer gardens and disco joints were all packed to the brim. Child prostitutes—of both sexes—still plied their wares along Cubao side streets and Quezon Boulevard, while an even brisker business went on in the cocktail lounges of downtown Manila.

With the scent of victory in the air, preparations were under way for the inauguration of Corazon C. Aquino. Enrile and Ramos suggested that it be held at Camp Crame, said Homobono Adaza later, and that the new government hold office there. "We decided that was not possible," Adaza said, "because the civilian part of the government would look like a captive of the military. We'd look like creatures of the military. But you know what the suggestion was from Mrs. Aquino's ward leaders? That she should be inaugurated at the Cojuangco Building or the Quezon City Sports Complex! I had to argue and argue again. It couldn't be in either place because we would have had to divide the Enrile-Ramos forces. It had to be outside Camp Crame but within its defense perimeter. Otherwise, with our military force halved, we would have been easy pickings for Marcos. I chose Club Filipino because it was near Camp Crame, because of its historical significance, and because of its name."

In the Palace, as the night deepened, things quieted down. What grounds keepers were left checked the state of the lawn, the trimmed bushes, the flowers, and the trees—which they had cared for for nearly twenty years, since the "Ma'am" liked only, in her own words, "the beautiful and the good." The Palace flora were now in a sorry state, trampled by combat boots and whatnot. Toward midnight, the

Palace grounds suffered even more when the gates were opened to a slew of ex-convicts, members of fanatic groups, and thugs of the Marcos's neighborhood associations.

Having lost the military power that had kept him in office for twenty years, Marcos had the brilliant idea of using his enemies' own tactic: he would assemble his own "people power" within the Palace—"the right solution," Irwin Ver, the general's son, had said over television. But the Marcos followers could only slip into Malacanang under cover of darkness, "thieves in the night," said a student who was keeping vigil at Nagtahan. But if the night had its demons, it also had its archbishop. Jaime Cardinal Sin, in disguise, was making the rounds of the city.

TEN

*A Farewell
to Marcos*

The crowd massed at EDSA was receiving warnings of an impending attack. Toti and Alicia had found each other again; worn out as much by the physical as by the emotional stress of the second day of their vigil, they had fallen asleep on newspaper sheets spread out on what was left of the grass near the Camp Crame walls. It had been Toti's idea to bury themselves deep in the crowd, he later said— that way, before the "enemy" reached them, they would at least be forewarned.

It was difficult to fall asleep, what with all the commotion, but after a while, first Alicia, then her brother drifted off. In the few moments that he remained awake, Toti said he thought of what would come next, what would happen to him, where he was going. He had sold nothing in the last twenty-four hours, and though he kept his money wadded carefully and tucked into a secret pocket in his waistband, he was feeling quite uneasy.

At the Palace, sleep escaped the besieged First Family as well. Both President and Mrs. Marcos were on the phone calling Washington in search of the drowning man's straw. Marcos spoke to Sen. Paul Laxalt, who had become a friend while visiting Manila before, while Mrs. Marcos was speaking to Nancy Reagan. Both had the same question: What did the U.S. president mean exactly by his statement? Perhaps Mr. Reagan meant that Marcos could stay on until 1987 if he were willing to share power with the opposition. Mrs. Marcos asked Mrs. Reagan just what the U.S. president was trying to imply in his public statement about the "current regime." The two Washington parties promised to check with the president and call back.

The subtle pressure that the U.S. embassy had exerted was beginning to tell. It was the old tactic of the hard and soft line; the embassy had thundered threats at Marcos to keep him in check while offering a way out and refuge to the women. The embassy personnel had worked on the women tirelessly, calling them up with repeated come-ons to the white beaches of Hawaii. "No one except the immediate family would know what they thought that terrible Sunday when everything failed," said a Marcos associate, "though I heard that the women were terrified and just wanted to be done with the whole thing. When you're not used to extreme pressure, when you've grown up protected or spent most of your life in comfort, you can't absorb stress. But imagine how humiliating it must have been for Marcos, who'd never lost in anything. To be the first Philippine head of state to have been overthrown." That, of course, merely rounded off his string of "firsts": first at the bar exams, youngest to have been elected president, first to have been reelected, first to have stayed thirteen years beyond his official term of office.

At one o'clock on Tuesday morning, a group of students keeping vigil near Nagtahan decided on their own psychological warfare tactic. They exploded a bunch of firecrackers, which startled the nodding soldiers, who began shooting, discharging their weapons into the air. Bullets flew all over the bridge, and the five hundred or so men and women keeping vigil there had to cower for cover. From time to time, though, they hurled stones and empty bottles at the troops. Because of the distance, most of the missiles fell on the bridge, which rapidly lost its usual well-kept look. But the incident must have jangled the nerves of the troops within the immediate vicinity of the Palace, for they kept on intermittently shooting at nothing. They could not have known that the noise was making the First Family even more jittery. By morning, nine people had been hit by aimless bullets and by shrapnel.

At EDSA, several false alarms stirred the defenders of the barricades, but otherwise the night passed unremarkably. There was a definite feeling of triumph. A nun said that since the rebellion had lasted this long, there was no reason why it couldn't last longer. But mostly people were relaxed, having weathered almost everything Marcos could throw at them. It was only a matter of time and method before he was pried out of the Palace.

Dawn was breaking when the call from Washington reached the Marcoses. Marcos, worn out by sleeplessness, nonetheless managed to surprise Senator Laxalt: he asked him directly if the U.S. president wanted him to step down. Laxalt said that that was not within President Reagan's right to demand. Then Marcos asked the senator, "What do you think? Should I step down?" Later the senator explained that he had not felt himself hampered by rules of diplomacy and could speak frankly. "I think you should cut and cut clean. The time has come." There was a godawful silence; the senator was prompted to ask, "Mr. President, are you still there?"

Marcos said yes, he was still there. "I'm so very, very disappointed," he said.

Nor was there comfort in Nancy Reagan's words to Mrs. Marcos. If there were no violence, the Marcoses and their entourage could come live in the United States. Mrs. Marcos reportedly took this answer with a modicum of grace.

It was a strange ending to a twenty-year romance. By bluster, by wheedling, by giving way, and by making the

United States invest so much in his regime, Marcos had kept Washington on his side all these long years. "But he had always thought that if the end were to come," said a Marcos associate, "it would come from the U.S." Later, I would hear the wildest explanations from Marcos people for the withdrawal of American support. Mrs. Marcos, said one, was well liked by the Arabs, and since Americans didn't like Arabs, they let Marcos be overthrown. Another believed that the all-encompassing corruption of the regime had been instigated and carried out by Central Intelligence Agency moles. In an ultimate exercise in self-exculpation, Marcos men ascribed the regime's fall to everything but the regime itself. Homobono Adaza, the Mindanao politician, who had fought Marcos for more years than he liked to remember, could still shake his head over the indignity of his fall. "He was a brilliant politician," Adaza said. "It takes many generations to breed a politician like Marcos. But he had the wrong values, the wrong orientation. If only he had had the right ones, he would have scintillated. Scintillated, I tell you."

The wrong values seemed still to be in operation that morning of his last day. Marcos must have acknowledged his defeat around this time—but he gave no indication of his coming abdication. On the national highway, crowds were still battling the tanks of the Fifth Infantry Division, which was trying to reach Manila. In Central Luzon, men and women were playing tag with the troops of Gen. Antonio Palafox. Later the tanks stalled at the North Expressway to the city, where defecting pilots from the Basa Air Force Base crippled them with rockets.

Corazon C. Aquino's inauguration had been set for eight in the morning, but as an impromptu affair, it was delayed for two hours. The lag gave Marcos an opportunity for one last try. He called Defense Minister Enrile. How could they settle the problem? The minister had no idea. Marcos then asked if it would be possible to organize a provisional government. "I just want a graceful exit." He would cancel the election results, set up a provisional government, and remain as honorary president until 1987. "I'd like to leave politics in a clean and orderly manner," Marcos said. Could he discuss that with Mrs. Aquino? Marcos was, in effect, begging.

The defense minister said it was too late; he and his men were committed to Mrs. Aquino. In the first place, Enrile demurred, they had not been interested in power, in setting up a military junta or a military government. Marcos then asked if he could leave the country safely. Enrile assured him that no one on his side wished the president any harm. Could he return safely sometime? Why not? Enrile said; this was his homeland, after all. Marcos, pressing his luck, asked if the same would hold true for General Ver. Enrile honestly replied that that was something he could not answer at the moment.

The inauguration that Adaza had wanted was here at last. Club Filipino, which had not foreseen this signal honor, was jammed tight with Mrs. Aquino's followers and campaign leaders, mostly the half-breed wealthy caste of the country. But the crowd was so huge that it spilled over to the outside, forming a protective barrier about the building. Soldiers of the mutiny were directing traffic around and away from the club and reconnoitering for danger all over the place. For once, the sight of guns and uniforms did not faze anyone, and the crowd was generally celebratory.

Inside the club, the normally circumspect rich were gaily raucous, standing on chairs, hailing one another and smiling, smiling, smiling. The hour of their return to power had come at last. Mrs. Aquino wore her standard yellow dress and horn-rimmed eyeglasses; she looked barely kempt, having driven over to the club from a nearby subdivision, where she had been hiding at a sister's house. Ramos and Enrile arrived by helicopter.

The invocation was delivered by Auxiliary Bishop Teodoro Bacani. Then Supreme Court Justice Vicente Abad Santos administered the oath of office to Vice President-elect Salvador H. Laurel, whose wife held the Bible for his vow. Laurel pledged "to work as I have never worked before." The audience broke into applause. But it held its breath for the climax as Mrs. Aquino rose and faced Supreme Court Justice Claudio Teehankee. She raised her right hand, placed her left on a Bible held by her husband's mother, Doña Aurora Aquino, and took her oath of office. The club nearly exploded from the audience's cheers; not a few burst into tears. Swiftly, President Aquino named Enrile her defense minister and Ramos her chief of staff. She also promoted the latter to full general. More applause. She delivered a short and simple speech, saying in part, "We became exiles in our own land—we Filipinos who are only at home in freedom—when Marcos destroyed the Republic fourteen years ago. Through the power of the people, we are home again."

Before the Aquino inauguration, Colonel Isleta had told Ramos that he thought "it was time to take Channel 9." It was Marcos's only remaining television station, and its loss would cripple his propaganda effort. Not that that was working, but taking the station at this time would draw Marcos's soldiers' attention from the ceremonies at Club Filipino. So early in the morning, Colonel Santiago, who was at Channel 4, heard staccato of gunfire coming from Channel 9. Unlike the other stations' takeovers, there were no negotiations here, no reasonableness. As part of the Channel 4 crowd accompanied the attacking soldiers to Channel 9, the Marcos forces inside opened fire.

Ferdinand E. Marcos's inauguration was scheduled for high noon. A Palace grounds supervisor said he walked around to check up on things because the stage, which had been built nonstop for three days, was no longer to be used. The ceremonies would be in Maharlika Hall. But there were now about two thousand men and women on the Palace grounds lunching on catered food—Marcos followers, the media, and soldiers. All the Marcos women wore white—Imelda and Imee wore the white *terno*, the traditional long gown of Filipinas, while Irene had on a white suit. Son Bongbong wore tailored combat fatigues. The rest, apart from the military men, wore the traditional *barong*, or white shirt. The family seemed undisturbed; there was no hint of their state of mind. The women kept smiling; their looks were regal, their gestures gracious. In this last public appearance, they would yet be aristocratic. As the government announcer said, "And now, the moment we have been waiting for," and Chief Justice Ramon Aquino asked Marcos to raise his right hand, and as Marcos did indeed raise his hand, a sniper aboard a helicopter hovering over Channel 9 fired his M-16 and hit the tower's main cable. Television sets all over the city blanked out.

In complete isolation from the rest of the country, the Marcoses went on with the futile ceremony. Afterward, President and Mrs. Marcos appeared at a balcony on the administration building and as snipers to the right and left of them trained rifles on the crowd below, the two sang a duet. In the garden, the tiny gathering waved little paper Philippine flags—blue, red, and yellow. Later the president mingled with his guests. With the walls about them, with the military standing guard, and with the opulence of the Palace—which had been the Spanish Governor-General's summer residence—on display, the Marcos loyalists could barely accept the rebellion as real.

Danilo Galang was back at the Palace area. He had tried to take photographs of the soldiers stationed near the Philippine Refining Company. But he had had the fright of his life when they raised their rifles and aimed them straight at him. Malacanang was a sorry sight, he said, even though the presidential security had expanded its defense perimeter by 1.5 kilometers. At Mendiola Bridge, the desultory participants of the Marcos inauguration were being heckled by the crowd as they tried to escape. "The crowd pelted them with coins of all denominations," said Galang. "The marines at the machine-gun nest on Mendiola Bridge then waved for them to retreat. Meanwhile, the police outside the Mendiola perimeter had turned congenial. They were encouraging the crowd to occupy areas close to the barricades because they'd heard that more Bayan members would be there shortly." The students in the crowd also went on exploding firecrackers and pelting the soldiers with pebbles and whatever missiles they could find.

Over at EDSA, the soldiers guarding Camp Aguinaldo simply disappeared. Enrile, who had fallen asleep after Aquino's inauguration—"I was so tired"—was awakened by his men. They were moving back to their old haunt; whatever threat had been there before had melted away. So the minister found himself in his old office once again. There another press conference was held. At approximately five o'clock, Marcos called Enrile up. Would he please stop those people "who are firing at the Palace towards our direction"? Enrile was surprised; he did not have any men, he said, in the area, but he would ask General Ramos to look into the matter. Marcos then said, "Will you please contact Ambassador Bosworth and ask him if he could make Teddy Allen and his group available to be my security escort? I want to leave the Palace." Enrile agreed.

Near Malacanang Palace at the Nagtahan Bridge area, a disturbance was taking place. The Marcos followers who could not cross Mendiola were trying to exit there, but the incensed crowd was pelting them with stones. "The troops on the other side of the barricades were being heckled," Galang recalled. "But behind the trestles, farther up J. P. Laurel street, there were children playing, oblivious to the danger." Nevertheless, the anger here and in downtown Manila was darker, the people ready to die. If there had been some certainty that even a few would survive an attempt to cross that divide to the Palace, the crowd would have done so simply for the pleasure of roaring into Marcos's face. Smoke from burning tires oozed into the streets and into the residential houses flanking the Palace.

It was seven o'clock already, about the time the U.S. ambassador was informing Aquino that Marcos was leaving. The actual exodus took place nearly an hour later. The family was ferried across the Pasig River to a spot where Clark Air Force Base helicopters could pick them up. "I saw a squadron of Sikorskys and Hueys headed northwest as the sun was setting," Galang said. Some said the delay had been caused by Mrs. Marcos's refusal to leave without Deputy Minister Jose Conrado Benitez; others said it was because Marcos needed medical attention and even had to be sedated. Arturo Tolentino steadfastly maintained later that Marcos had been either abducted or removed from the Palace by deceit. "He agreed to be taken to Ilocos," he said, "but at Clark he was told there were orders for him to be taken to Hawaii. I have the impression that the trip was a sudden one, without the knowledge and consent of the U.S. president."

Fr. Jose Dizon was back at Nagtahan that evening. "So many people wanted to rush the Palace already," said the priest, "but we tried to hold them back." He, Leto Villar, and other leaders of the cause-oriented groups conferred on what to do. "The commanding officer of the unit at Gate Two said his men wanted to surrender, but they were afraid they would be lynched by the mob. So there was this big problem: How do you bring the soldiers out? I thought since there were a number of us priests there, we'd wake up whoever was at nearby San Beda College and ask if they could give sanctuary to the soldiers for the evening. So we did that, and the San Beda people agreed to take them.

"First, of course, we had to disarm the soldiers. We told them, 'If the people see you carrying those guns, they might go after your throats.' We took all their guns, promising to return them afterward. Now, as we were escorting them to San Beda, Colonel Garcia told us that there were other forces within the Palace grounds. And these were determined to kill anyone who entered. They were ex-convicts—Marcos fanatics, who'd been at the inauguration that morning."

Hearing this, the priests and other organizers held the people back. "We tried to negotiate with the men inside the Palace," he said. "Waldy Carbonell got a megaphone and called out to them, saying, 'We're all Filipinos here, choose a leader so we can parlay.' But a loud voice replied, 'If you want to enter, enter, but we will kill you!' A man came over to us and said he was an employee of the Palace and only fanatics remained inside." Even the grounds keepers had sought refuge in the covered manholes in the streets and within the Palace grounds. "Hearing this, we got even more worried and kept trying to tell the people to keep back."

Camp Crame learned about the departure only thirty minutes after the Marcoses had left. "I saw Minister Enrile and General Ramos really furious," said Colonel Isleta. "By that time, we heard that people were already rushing the Palace. The minister and the general cried out, 'Why couldn't they coordinate with us if they were leaving? Then there could have been a formal transfer of power and things would have been orderly. If only they had coordinated with us.' " *They* presumably meant the U.S. embassy.

"We were able to keep the crowd at bay for only thirty minutes more," said Father Dizon, "by which time Ramos's men had already secured the Palace proper. Then the crowd broke through the barricades, poured over the gate, opened it, and stormed the Administration Building." It was quick and explosive. A man brandishing a knife met the crowd head on; two men started pummeling a third. A man clambered hand over hand up the balcony where the First Couple had sung their swan song. He seized the flag draped by its side and peppered it with kisses. Inside the building, people were running up and down the corridors and into rooms, tearing down the paraphernalia of Marcos's rule. Sheaves of paper came floating out of windows like doves; the portraits followed, the oil paintings of the "Sir" and the "Ma'am" that had been paid for with thousands of dollars. The crowd below let loose a bloodcurdling roar and began hitting the portraits, again and again. Finally, they set them on fire and danced out their rage around the flames.

Only a few managed to get into the Palace proper, among them a group of American journalists. Charlyn Zlotnick, who'd smashed her camera lens, just kept walking and entering corridors and losing herself in the labyrinthine interior of the Palace. "I must have entered the inner-innermost sections," she said. "I didn't see anyone. There were no guards, or the few I saw ignored me. All the commotion was going on in the other building. Anyway, you know how they say that Mrs. Marcos would use a bar of soap only once? Well, I saw bushels and bushels of these expensive soap bars in the bathroom—and what looked like gallons of perfume. The terrible thing about it was that it never occurred to me—I mean, when I came out and met this other group of American photographers and writers, they asked me what I got. Every one of them had picked up a souvenir. And I had none."

The news spread like prairie fire through the city. Firecrackers went off, bells pealed, and at EDSA the weary crowd found a last burst of energy to weep, scream, dance, and cheer. The noise more than anything else woke Toti and Alicia up, and for a minute they could not understand what was going on, why the nuns and priests were cavorting as if possessed. But they caught on, caught on soon, and both started to laugh, gently at first, then louder and louder, bending over, bending backward, as nearly two million people went into hysterics. Unaware of what they were doing, the two street kids, dirty, ugly and stinking, joined hands, palm to palm, and began to turn around and around, chanting over and over again, "Wala na, wala na ('He's gone')!" In houses all over the city, adults and children rushed to get something to drink—water, beer, Coke, or wine; the rich popped champagne corks—for a last toast to Marcos: Thank God he's gone.

Danilo Galang was jerked from his sleep by this tremendous noise. Luis Teodoro remembered little of what happened except for a weird scene on television in which Gen. Prospero Olivas, who had long been a thorn in Ramos's side, was smiling and saying, "Our beloved president, Corazon Aquino."

Br. Cornelio Jaranilla, who'd kept vigil at EDSA, was at Channel 4 when the news came. Moved by impulse, he, two other brothers, and a Jesuit priest walked all the way to Camp Aguinaldo, passing cheering crowds. Then from Camp Aguinaldo they walked to the Palace. It didn't occur to them to find a ride, they were that ecstatic. They walked on and on, feeling no fatigue. "We wanted to see the Palace," said Jaranilla, "to make sure it was ours." There he was taken aback by the sight of portraits burning and flower hedges being trampled to bits and pieces. "I saw an old man pulling out a plant," said Jaranilla, "and when I asked him why, he said he was taking it home to his grandson, and he would tell him that the plant became his on the day Marcos left the Philippines."

Jaime Cardinal Sin was as agog over the developments as the rest of the country. "When I called on the people to protect Enrile and Ramos," he said, "all I was thinking of was to prevent bloodshed. I had no thought of ousting Marcos. But then he left!" The cardinal laughed.

Salvacion Bueno reached the Palace at ten in the evening with a covey of nuns. "In my entire life, this was the only time I ever set foot in the Palace," she said, "in my entire, whole life." And because a woman's work was never done, after picking up after the crowd at EDSA, there she was again, sweeping and picking up trash and cleaning—for oh, how terribly dirty this seat of power was! There were feces all over the place, where the Marcos people had relieved themselves, it was so awful. But for now, there was a moment of lightness sweeping through the nation, an amazement that *they* had done it, had accomplished this miracle: the blight was gone, the plague lifted.

ELEVEN

Epilogue

It was perfectly Zen, and only a people as unselfconsciously mystical as Filipinos could have carried it off. The fall of Marcos came about through a series of accidents, transforming what could have been certain defeat to victory. After the military's coup attempt snagged, Defense Minister Enrile and General Ramos had no choice but to let themselves be carried by the flow of events from hour to hour, day to day. Control was taken out of their hands and transferred to the crowd, which, having no leaders and no organizational structure, had no vulnerable spots, either. Nor did it have any concept of what it should do, based on classic rules of warfare. It only fixed its mind on the idea of avoiding bloodshed and thus keeping Marcos's camp and that of Enrile-Ramos apart.

The formal protagonists never even caught sight of one another. From their rigidly held static defensive positions, from the safety of their ramparts, they postured threateningly and hurled war challenges at each other, like roosters in a war dance before actual combat. Although the four days were fraught with moments that could have exploded into violence, the presence of millions—of men, women, and children—changed the quality of the confrontation. The people practiced perfect Zen, wielding the weapon of immobility against Marcos's attempts to push and shove them, the weapon of complete defenselessness against his assaults. Then finally they ignored him, canceling his very existence as a power. He had no choice except to leave, said a friend; for how do you go about ordering something as abstract and yet as real as The People?

Col. Honesto Isleta had one last recollection of those days. On the morning of the twenty-sixth, he said, General Ramos had gone off to take a nap. "We could not disturb him," he said, "even though an American anchorman sat in the office waiting to interview him on satellite television. Finally the American couldn't wait any longer, and he got up to go. Before leaving, though, he turned to me and said, 'Colonel, I just want to say this: I've covered revolutions all over the world; yours is a classic.' " Isleta smiled.

Arturo Tolentino said he "felt robbed."

The euphoria lasted two months. By April, it was interesting to watch people's faces in public buses whenever they entered a road named Marcos or passed a park named Imelda. Their eyes glanced at the letters, looked through the signs, and ignored them. Those names, which had ruled the country for twenty years, had become nothing more than hieroglyphics, an alien language. People were beginning to forget Marcos. The only persistence of his memory was in a small group that rallied daily at Rizal Park or picketed the U.S. embassy asking for his return. No one paid attention; cars passed by, and drivers cursed at the inconvenience. No one held it against them that they persevered in their affection for Marcos; like Mrs. Aquino, who'd said she could be magnanimous in victory, the people were magnanimous, too.

At the National Press Club, I watched an old newspaperman who'd led Marcos's propagandists hold court, perorate, and damn the new government. The young journalists, many of whom had been imprisoned, kicked out of their jobs, blacklisted, and harassed in every conceivable way, listened to him quietly, beer glasses in hand, wry smiles on their faces. Finally, as one was about to leave, he asked the Marcos journalist, "What do you have to complain about? You're rich, you're unharmed, you still have your job. When you were in power, you would not even let us breathe." There was laughter; people turned their backs.

Still later, a Marcos spokesman in Hawaii told me that a hate campaign against Marcos was being waged in Manila. One could not even begin to tell him the truth—that Filipinos wanted to forget Marcos, wanted not to think of him anymore, and more than anything else wanted to get on to problems more pressing than the fate of an old, deposed, sick dictator. As far as they were concerned, he and his wife belonged now to the never-never land of the stuff of legends: Marcos's hollow machismo and Imelda's thousand pairs of shoes. The only aspects of the Marcos regime that still concerned them were the problems of retrieving the wealth the Marcoses had purloined and of making sure that such a regime never ruled the Philippines again.

Homobono Adaza, for his part, saw the present as a "transition period" and the bellicose personalities who had taken over the government as "transitional figures." He quoted former Sen. Benigno Aquino to the effect that the true government that would succeed the Marcos regime would be a government not controlled by the oligarchy, "and the messiah that the country waits for would be a leader coming from the masses of the Filipino people." He believed in that firmly, with no reservations.

Br. Cornelio Jaranilla brought out of the four-day experience a consciousness of himself as a citizen of the country. "Before this, I did not give a damn, so long as my own family was all right," he said. "But during that election, I realized that indeed evil was present in our society, along with good. I am now in the world. I tell myself to be patient, to wait; change will not happen overnight." In small ways, he tries to maintain the stand he took during those four days.

After the fall, he got his driver's license from a government agency. For an extra one hundred fifty pesos, the examiner told him, he could have a license in two hours. Otherwise, he would have to wait. Brother Jaranilla refused, telling the man that he supported good government. "I waited eight hours to take the exam," he said, "and saw so many paying up. I felt personally aggrieved. After all the effort—" Still, he tries to follow politics more closely now and to be critical in his view of government, feeling that he has a stake in it.

The sudden and wholesale involvement of people in the affairs of government is one result of the EDSA rebellion. Peasants march to the Palace. The urban poor take their grievances directly to the great white way of Nagtahan and Mendiola. Students and teachers refuse to accept directives without question. Provincial and local constituencies demand to be heard in the choice of their officials. Women mount campaigns against high prices, pornography, and other issues distressing to their gender.

An active and politically aware populace is not always palatable to those who govern, especially when they believe themselves wiser and more knowledgeable than those who can't speak English and have no titles. Still, if democracy is the intent, this is a welcome development. As the years of the Marcos regime showed, general passivity is a fertile ground for dictatorship.

But although the populace became politicized overnight, the military also became politicized—in the wrong sense of the word. It emerged from February 1986 conscious of its own power—a genie, as it were, let out of the bottle. The present problem—and a pressing one for any civilian government—is how to return it to its former status as an "implementor" rather than a maker of policy.

The military had kept itself intact, in the name of solidarity for the sake of solidarity, by refusing to purge itself of human rights violators and pro-Marcos elements and by refusing even to punish thoroughly those involved in the constant agitation for Marcos's return. It continues to hold itself as a separate entity, apart from the nation, apart from the government. Gen. Fidel Ramos, say some reporters who cover defense, may not be the right person to lead the military back to its proper niche as subordinate to the civilian government. Although he is an efficient soldier, accomplishing assigned tasks with the minimum of fuss, he has no originality, they say, and has never been one to initiate anything new. His main concern has been the preservation of the military as a structure, independent of politics—a difficult thing to do in this era of post-Marcos polarization.

What is necessary, the reporters say, is the politicization of the military in the right way. That is, it must understand politics in terms of principle and not in terms of personal leadership. Such a move would be vigorously opposed by the young officers, who have seen how the institution can became a means for the attainment of personal power and privilege. The military remains the country's biggest problem, the single biggest source of instability; and it promises to remain that way for years to come.

President Corazon C. Aquino has brought to the country her own style of leadership, including an excruciatingly slow approach to problem solving. Some say this style is not intrinsic but rather grows out of her own and her advisers' inexperience, as well as out of the lack of a common perspective of the national situation and what to do about it.

Certainly, the problems are enormous. Marcos left the country with early-maturing loans of $30 billion at high interest rates; he left the country physically devastated, its roads in ruins, and Metro-Manila in decay. The political compromises that shored up his regime for twenty years became institutionalized, from corruption to warlordism. The central government was weakened, and the law does not operate in many areas of the archipelago. The military itself taught the people over and over again for 14 years that the Constitution is merely a piece of paper on which words have been printed. Other means of empowerment are necessary if the Constitution is to become meaningful to those who are poor and anonymous.

Mrs. Aquino herself practices a form of feudal political

patronage. She appoints her ministers and officials on the basis of her friendship with and political indebtedness to them. She can be inflexible and intolerant of criticism, and when confronted with complaints she often breaks out in irascible reminders of what she is owed by those who complain. Since the country needs more than ever an efficient administration, these traits could work against her rule.

Marcos also left the country with a seventeen-year-old insurgency—although his regime exacerbated its root causes rather than bred them. The revolution led by the National Democratic Front is the latest phase of a four-hundred-year peasant revolt for control of the country's prime asset—land. The problem has become critical with a high birth rate and population growth, and with the shrinking of job opportunities in the cities. The domination of the current government by the traditional landed gentry gives little hope that property relations in the country will be changed, or that the tiny archipelago will at last industrialize to create the wherewithal to support its burgeoning population. One keeps one's fingers crossed, hoping that "Christian values" will impose their own restraints on greed.

From my talks with the leadership of the underground, it is clear to me that there will be no abandonment of the agrarian basis of the revolution; that no matter what, the demands of the peasantry will remain primal. Even the question of the U.S. bases can be solved through negotiations, but definitely and absolutely the ancient cry of the landless tillers for land will constitute the cornerstone of the underground's decisions vis-à-vis the new government. And if necessary the underground will wage war for seventeen more years until this basic problem is resolved once and for all.

Still, hope persists, even for a population whose back is to the wall; and the rich are attempting, tentatively and willy-nilly, to reach out of their enclaves of opulence to listen to the poor. In the summer of 1986 a number of benefit-dinners were held in the country's ritziest houses for former political prisoners, 90 percent of whom came from the lower classes. There the faces of the comfortable stared curiously at those who spoke of their travails in Marcos's prisons and of why they had embarked on the road to resistance. Comically, only one question—phrased in many different ways—was asked of the poor by the rich: If you win, will you kill us? It was in a way an acknowledgment of their responsibility in what had happened, as well as the beginning of a consciousness of themselves as citizens of this country, not of some floating nation of jet-setters.

Within that same period, I witnessed a different kind of gathering; Selda, the society of former detainees, held its first congress. What I saw there made me doubt that the chasm between the classes, polarized as they had been by the Marcos regime, could ever be bridged. It was a deeply moving reunion of those who had been tortured and imprisoned; there were gaps among the familiar faces. The disappeared, the executed, would never surface again. But at that moment, each of those who had gone into the detention camps could nourish his or her spirit on the fact that many did survive, that this many, after all, outlived the regime itself. The trick now, said one, was to outlive Marcos himself. They, the former prisoners, were living memorials of what the regime had been, and as long as one was alive, he or she would be a witness. But would that wisdom be comprehensible to those who had no idea of what constituted suffering?

Salvacion Bueno stayed at the Palace for ten months, cleaning and sweeping, waiting for a promised job. In all that time, she received payment only twice. Then abruptly, because she and the others were supposedly "volunteers," she was told to leave. The poor, as she says, are indispensable in moments of crisis and are dispensable in times of stability. But she never regretted joining the four-day rebellion, because she did it in the name of freedom. Next time, though, she said, she will stay at home, since she knows now that whether governments rise or fall, her life remains the same.

Danilo Galang returned to teaching, as did Monico

Atienza. Luis Teodoro turned over his office at the President's Center for Special Studies to men of the new government and assumed open editorship of the ecumenical news service that he and his friends had put together and kept alive all through the Marcos years.

Malacanang Palace has become a tourist spot that the people can visit free of charge, except on Wednesdays, when the president holds her cabinet meetings there. There is always a throng outside, mostly of the "rubber-sandals" crowd, standing under the hot sun to ogle what had been the living quarters of the First Family. It is suffocatingly enclosed, this Palace, not at all the river-breeze-swept building of my childhood recollection. There is a quasi-throne room, complete with two massive carved wooden chairs upholstered in red velvet, for the "Sir" and the "Ma'am." Marcos's bedroom is ascetic, with bare wooden floors, a hospital bed, and oxygen tanks, as well as air filters. Mrs. Marcos's bedroom is a rather dim, cavernous chamber without windows; her bed is canopied with lace curtains that rise to a cupola in the ceiling. Outside, the kitchen looks like any suburban kitchen, with copper kettles and pans on the wall. The dining room is austere, while in the private prayer room a collection of antique reliquaries stands. A statue or two allegedly had been stolen from churches.

On the floor below, reachable by way of a winding narrow staircase, was the boutique, housing row upon row of gowns, shoes, bags, and fur coats for Mrs. Marcos. She must have gained weight since my last sight of her, judging by their size. Off to one side was the treasure room, where cartons of designer shirts still in their plastic wrapping were found, along with strings of seed pearl and gold chain necklaces, bottles of perfume and aftershave, and all kinds of knickknacks from abroad, all brand new and unopened. Marita Manuel told me that whenever Mrs. Marcos returned from a trip, she would call her Blue Ladies, the daughters and wives of millionaires, alumnae of the best finishing schools in Switzerland. They would come over, and she would talk to them and talk to them and talk to them, keeping them beyond the bounds of their own patience—and only at the very last minute, at the very last instant, would she call out to her aide to bring the things she'd brought home for the girls. Then the aide would appear with an armful of this stuff and dump it on the floor, causing the women to scramble and shriek and grab as Mrs. Marcos watched, a slight smile playing about her lips. In more ways than one, she was a product of the country's inexorable caste system that had ostracized her when she and her family had been poor; thus it had ignited the vengeful obsession with wealth with which she later swindled the entire country.

There was a small hospital room in the Palace and four or five portable dialysis machines, state-of-the-art models, that could not be found in any of the country's hospitals. There was even a dentist's office and, of course, innumerable oil paintings of the "Sir" and the "Ma'am," no one else's, as if they could not stand to see any other face immortalized. There were art objects mixed in with the tackiest of knickknacks. And there were, of course, boxes of soap and gallon bottles of perfume. Although the military claimed that the Palace had been looted, it appeared for the most part intact; the minute evidence of the Marcoses' existence was still in place. The Marcoses must have derived some comfort from the thought that Malacanang has remained a virtual memorial-tomb of their reign—except that, as with tombs, the Palace was redolent with the quality of the unreal, the ancient, the no-longer viable.

Maintaining the Palace, which had been centrally air-conditioned by the Marcoses, is a headache; so too is maintaining some forty-five other residences that the Marcoses had built, or that were built for them by sycophants—houses of all shapes and sizes, in all kinds of locales, over which the old caretakers still watch, drawing their pay from the national budget. They are empty; some were lived in for only two weeks, and all are a curious combination of that tacky elegance and "ethnicity" that the Marcoses seem to have loved. Apart from the houses, there is also son Bong-bong's "safari island," where African animals roam; Mrs. Marcos's buildings, which are slowly settling into the reclaimed land at Manila Bay; and the various museums housing Ferdinand Marcos paraphernalia in his home province and Mrs. Marcos's paraphernalia in her home province. Although the new government has decided to keep his Great Stone Face in the north intact, one can only have so much of Marcos relics.

Outside in the blistering equatorial light, life goes on as usual. The Marcos partisans maintain their favorite haunts, among them the Intercontinental Hotel coffee shop, where the suety gentlemen of the old regime meet and posture and talk about a return to power. In the universities and in the church, the endless debates still go on as to what has to be done and where the country is going. An air of tentativeness remains, a feeling that nothing has been completed although there is the chance to do so. And in the streets the children, dirtier and more numerous, go on plying their wares, hustling from dawn to dusk, unsure whether they really exist. Unemployment in Metro-Manila stands at nearly 40 percent and businesses that folded during the Marcos regime remain closed. The gutted buildings of the economic crisis are unrefurbished, and despite the government's attempts to draw in foreign investments, the situation is not stable enough to attract capital from overseas.

Still, there is laughter, the kind let loose by a people whose sense of the absurd has been honed by history. Already, in cocktail lounges and theaters, the fall of Marcos and all the elements thereof are fast becoming ridiculous. Bump-and-grind singers croon the inspirational songs of the FebReb (short for February rebellion) libidinously, while the beer-drinking crowd hollers, "Take it off!" Plays create improbable scenes of reconciliation, in which Marcos arrives at the Manila International Airport, pees in his pants, and dies on the very tarmac where former Sen. Benigno Aquino died. Relentless, the lampooning goes on—on stage, in films, on television—as Filipinos, knowing that the things they hold dear have been and can be taken away from them, seek to propitiate the gods by vulgarizing their only victory in four hundred years. It is pathetic.

Jaime Cardinal Sin lapsed into uncharacteristic silence after the fall of Marcos. Many of the religious said that in hindsight, their own strength and power in the rebellion had worried them. They had become too much of the world, and they now sought to make amends by withdrawing, allowing those whose function in life is to administer the temporal realm to take over. Nevertheless, they remain quietly aware of what they can do and of the necessary circumspection with which they should use their own capability to affect developments in the country.

Toti and Alicia, scarcely older than they were when the whole furor took place, resumed their lives of quiet desperation, one selling cigarettes, the other flower garlands. From EDSA, they finally went home at midnight on the twenty-fifth, loaded with leftover foodstuffs from the nuns, only to find their shack empty. The whole family had rushed to the streets to celebrate Marcos's fall—and by luck, the two urchins escaped punishment for having disappeared during those days without a word to anyone. Like the nameless millions who stood at EDSA and Malacanang those four days, all Toti and Alicia brought out of the experience were their own stories; perhaps they will be told and retold, when the two are older, to their own children and grandchildren. The day after the fall of Marcos, they were back at their posts, not even aware they had done something momentous.

They had joined without hope of reward, had struggled without a stake in the outcome of the battle, and having done their bit, had returned to anonymity. They are there— along with children who look like them, stunted, burned black by the sun, their clothes limned in carbon monoxide and soot—in the streets of Manila. It seems improbable that heroes can be forged from such material, that some of the most decisive moves in the endgame against the Marcos regime were made by them and their kind.

Index

Marcos, 187; pastoral letters of, 101, 102; and post election scenarios, 111; profile of, 100–101; and Radio Veritas, 100; and union of Marcos' opposition, 43

Sison, Jose Ma., 60, 78; and announcement of coup, 125

Sister Bobbie, 146

"Snap" election, 31, 57

Social Security System, 29

Somiya, Ambassador Kikoshi, 116

Sorce, Wayne, 32–33, 39, 44

Sotelo, Col. Antonio, 154

Station DZRB, 133

Sugar barons, 18

Sumulong, 78

Tadiar, Gen. Artemio, 145, 146

Tañada, Sen. Lorenzo, 4, 39; at EDSA, 135–136

Tao, *xi*

TAPAT, 85

Tavera, Mita Pardo de, 25

Thanksgiving Day, and martial law day, 23

Teehankee, Justice Claudio, 170

Teodoro, Luis, 24, 162, 184; and coup, 118; and meeting with Cristobal, 138–139; and move from University campus, 153; and view of Marcos regime, 28–29

Tolentino, Arturo, 46, 173; on Aquino-Laurel agreement, 101; on 1986 election, 95–96; and offer to mediate, 161; and RAM coup

Trade Union Council of Philippines, 120

Transportation strike of 1972, 2

Underground: development of, 77–78; after Marcos, 182; recruitment for, 77

Unemployment, after Marcos, 186

UNIDO: defined, 10; and support for Laurel, 42–43

United Democratic Opposition, 5

United Democratic Party. *See* UNIDO

United States: and departure of Marcos, 172; and Marcos' threats, 102; and Marcos' war records, 55; observers at election, 99; presence during 1986 election, 55; and pressure for elections, 86; and relations with Philippines, 67–68

United States embassy: and knowledge of coup, 115; and pressure on Marcos, 166

United States naval bases, 102: after Marcos, 182

University Belt, 152

University of Life, 134

University of Philippines, 18, 134

Untold Story of Imelda Romualdez-Marcos (Pedrosa), 17

U.S.S. Enterprise, 55

Ver, Gen. Fabian, 3, 145; and "all out" force defence, 162; and Aquino murder, 33; criticized by PMA, 33; and delay of author's passport, 37; and Enrile conflict, 34–35, 37, 39; and Enrile/Ramos coup, 126–127; 1985 leave of absence of, 34; profile of, 35–36; and red-alert, 105; reorganization plan of, 34; "resignation" of (Marcos), 109; trial of, 4

Ver, Irwin, 36, 128; and "right solution," 164

Versoza, Eubolio, 155, 158–159

Vidal, Ricardo Cardinal, 107

Vietnam War: and CPP, 62; and Philippine involvement, 16

Villar, Leto, 120, 173

Way, The (Tao), *xi*

We Belong Movement, 33–34

Weinberger, Caspar, 161

World Bank, 31

Yñiguez, Nicanor, 104

Zlotnick, Charlyn, 143; at Aquinaldo, 123–124, 129; and campaign of 1986, 50–51; at Palace seizure, 174–175
Zobel, Jaime, 131